From Blueberries to Wild Roses

A Northwoods Wild Foods Cookbook

By Dottie Reeder

Explorer's Guide Publishing
Rhinelander, WI

From Blueberries to Wild Roses
A Northwoods Wild Foods Cookbook

Copyright© Dottie Reeder

All rights reserved. No part of this book may be reproduced in any form or by any means, electronic or mechanical, including photocopying, recording or by an information storage or retrieval system without written permission from the publisher, except for inclusion of brief quotations in a review.

First Edition, 1995
Printed in the United States of America

Published by
 Explorer's Guide Publishing
 4843 Apperson Drive
 Rhinelander, WI 54501
 (715) 362-6029

ISBN 1-879432-15-3

Library of Congress Catalog Card Number: 94-61838

Limits of Liability and Disclaimer of Warranty

This book was written to enrich your knowledge and appreciation of cooking with wild foods. The information presented within this book is not intended as an authority on the subject. The publisher and author shall have neither liability nor responsibility to any person or entity with respect to any loss or damage caused, or alleged to be caused, directly or indirectly by the information contained in this book.

This book is dedicated with love to the memory of two women, each named Catherine, who have had a tremendous influence on my life.

> Catherine (Kate) Macke, my maternal grandmother, who taught me how to bake a great loaf of bread, and how to live in the world.

> Catherine (Todell) Reeder, my mother-in-law, who taught me that gourmet cooking is really just basic country cooking using fresh ingredients, and who taught her family the importance of good food, good company and good values.

Contents

INTRODUCTION		v
1	Wild Foods	1
2	Appetizers	17
3	Beverages	27
4	Breads	35
5	Salads	49
6	Soups	59
7	Entrées	69
8	Vegetables	83
9	Desserts	95
10	Miscellaneous	109
INDEX		119

Introduction

One of my fondest childhood memories is that of picking blackberries near my home in High Ridge, Missouri. The beautiful, tasty berries grew near our home. On hot summer days, my sisters and I would pick those delectable berries and eat them, sweet and luscious, right off the vines.

The next memory that enters my mind in reference to wild foods is later in my life, at the age eighteen, when I met my future mother-in-law. She loved to walk, and she loved to gather wild greens as she walked, to prepare what she referred to as "a spring tonic". This consisted of tender young dandelion greens and poke sallet which grew abundantly near her cozy home in the Missouri countryside. She generously shared her knowledge with me and taught me to identify these plants easily.

Still later, I moved to beautiful Northern Wisconsin with my husband Sonny and our three children, Lyn, Tim and Shelly. Here I discovered the abundance of wild berries, greens, and nuts available and began to learn to identify them. Over the years this activity has provided many hours of outdoor enjoyment for me and for our family.

Country folks have always used wild plants as part of their diet, for medicinal purposes, for dyes, insect repellents, and scents. Unfortunately, most of these prized plants are considered weeds by the general population.

A stroll down any roadside or country path in the Northwoods of Wisconsin during the summer months will reveal the abundance of wild foods available. On a walk in mid-July I discovered lamb's quarter, dandelion, clover, raspberry, blackberry, blueberries, hazelnuts, juneberries, wild asparagus, rose petals, mint, false camomile, wintergreen, wild strawberries, Jerusalem Artichokes, and maple trees — most of which I used in the recipes for this book. These plants were all in different phases of growth, some ready to harvest, some beyond the harvest time, and some still ripening.

I am personally familiar with the plants used in these recipes. There are many, many more edible wild foods for the adventurous gourmet. Variety is said to be the spice of life and these foods certainly add a delightful variety to our diet. Usually these foods are very nutritious as well.

I can't stress enough the importance of correct plant identification. Remember that whenever you decide to harvest wild foods, you must be absolutely certain that you are picking the right plant. If you are ever unsure - don't eat it! Take a knowledgeable person with you in the beginning to help you identify the plants.

Another point to consider when harvesting wild foods is whether the plant is near an area that has been sprayed with pesticides. Usually, harvesting foods very near the roads and near power lines is not recommended. Also, if you decide to explore on private property, be sure to ask for permission from the owner first.

Most of the wild foods used here can be substituted by domestic foods. Usually, you will find domestic varieties are larger in size than the wild foods, especially in the case of berries. Fresh spinach can easily be substituted for dandelion or other wild greens.

So, take some time to walk through the woods and down country lanes. Learn to identify some wild foods. Experiment with them and enjoy a new adventure in eating. If you don't live near the woods or the country lanes, you can still enjoy the recipes in this book by substituting their domestic relatives.

Bon Appetit,

Dottie

Chapter 1
Wild Foods

Blackberries
Blueberries
Clover
Cranberries
Dandelion
Hazelnuts
Juneberries
Jerusalem Artichoke
Lamb's Quarter
Maple Syrup
Mint
Raspberries
Wild Rice
Wild Roses
Wild Strawberries

Blackberries

Blackberries are one of the most abundant berries found in the northwoods. They can be found throughout the United States. Similar to the raspberry, the blackberry is also high in Vitamin C.

Habitat: Blackberries are frequently found growing in moist and partially opened areas along field rows, forest edges, and logging or rural roads.

Characteristics: Blackberries are members of the rose family, and as such, their thorny canes can be just as treacherous. Early in the summer the plant sports a white, five petaled blossom. Berries are pale green in color and turn a deep purple-black upon ripening.

Harvesting: Blackberries can be harvested from late June to August. Pick these black jewels about two days after they have turned deep purple-black in color for the best taste. The berries should be refrigerated until ready to use. Wash and remove stems just before using.

Uses: The berries may be served fresh, in any number of tasty preparations, or make into syrups, jams, sauces, pies and baked goods. When cooked, blackberries turn red. Blackberry leaves may be used for brewing teas and potpourri.

Blueberries

The delicious blueberry is a favorite of Northwoods visitors and local residents alike. Many people are very secretive regarding the location of their favorite blueberry patch. In addition, blueberries are very nutritious. Just one cup of wild blueberries will provide up to $1/3$ of an adult's daily requirement of Vitamin C. The berries also contain Vitamin A, calcium, iron, magnesium, potassium, and zinc. And they are low in fat and calories.

Habitat: Called a pioneering plant, you'll find blueberries in abundance in sunny burned-over fields, cleared forest, and old pastures. They like acid soils especially were the lands have been recently disturbed.

Characteristics: Blueberries grow in small clusters on low bushes. When ripe, between July and September, the berries sometimes have a slight haze which can be easily washed off.

Harvesting: Blueberries should be left on the bush for several days to a week after they turn blue. A fully ripe berry will be slightly soft and sweet, and easily separate from the stem. When picked, these berries can be used fresh or frozen for later use. To freeze, spread berries in a single layer on a cookie sheet. Freeze, then place in freezer containers and return to freezer until used.

Uses: Blueberries can be used in pies, cobblers, syrups, and muffins. The leaves are sometimes used in teas and potpourri.

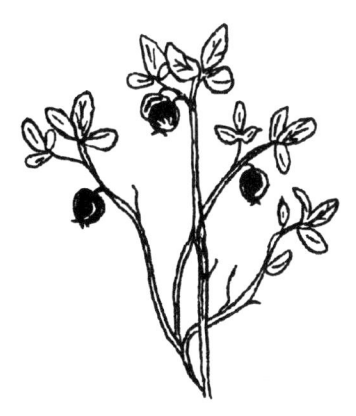

Red Clover & White Clover

One of the most delightful scents of summer is a field of clover blooming in the warm sun.

Habitat: This common plant appears along roadsides, in fields, and along the side of country roads.

Characteristics: Easily identified by its three leaves and pretty blossoms on top of a single stalk. There are three small stalks at the end of each the main stem. The blossoms may be a red, pink, or white color.

Harvesting: Pick the leaves when young and harvest the blossoms at full bloom. Rinse blossoms and leaves, dry, and store in refrigerator.

Uses: The leaves can be eaten raw, as fresh greens, or cooked. Blossoms, fresh or dried make a refreshing summer tea. Dried clover blossoms are also an excellent addition to potpourris.

Cranberries

These berries are one of only three major native North American fruits. They were very important to indigenous people in the making of pemmican, a food designed to last through the long winters. Cranberry festivals, throughout the Northwoods, celebrate the many wonderful ways to prepare this versatile native berry.

Habitat: Cranberries are grown in commercial bogs or can be found growing wild in marshy areas.

Characteristics: This plant is identified by it's thick oval shaped evergreen leaves on low shrubs and the pink or red flowers that blossom between June and late July. The berry initially is green, then turns red in late fall when it ripens. The fruit is edible raw, but is usually too tart to be eaten this way. It is best to pick the berries after the first frost.

Harvesting: In the commercial bogs, the plants are flooded then harvesting with "floating combines". In the wild, the fruit is hand picked and stored in porous containers (damp fruit will mold) in a cool place.

Uses: Cranberries are used to make juices, sauces, and relishes. They are a tasty addition to breads, puddings, and muffins as well. Recently, dried sweetened cranberries have been developed commercially, offering consumers a raisin-like cranberry, sometimes referred to as a Craisin.®

Dandelion

Usually looked upon as a weed, this common plant, found throughout the world, offers a great deal of nutritional value. It is rich in vitamins and minerals, especially high in Vitamin A. These plants were also used as a remedy for certain ailments.

Habitat: Dandelions can be found growing in sunny areas in almost any type of soil.

Characteristics: Leaves are long, dark green with jagged edges. A bright yellow flower can be found on the end of a long hollow stalk.

Harvesting: The leaves, roots, and flowers should be harvested when very young and tender, and used fresh. If you gather these greens too late in the season, you'll discover these mature leaves to be quite bitter.

Uses: The young leaves can be used as fresh greens. The young buds of the golden yellow flower are edible, and are sometimes used in salads or fritters. In early times, the flowers were used to make a yellow dye. Many wild food enthusiasts still prepare a tasty wine from the blossoms of this versatile plant. The roots may be used as a vegetable when scraped clean and boiled in water. When dried and roasted, these roots are sometimes used as a coffee substitute.

Hazelnuts

Hazelnuts and filberts belong to the same family. These tasty nuts are difficult to gather, because the chipmunks and squirrels love them as much as we do. They almost always get to the nuts before we can harvest them.

Habitat: These shrubs can be found along streams, forest edges, in the understorage area of large trees, and along roadsides.

Characteristics: The plants are shrubs with long branches and wide, spade-shaped leaves. The branches are seven to eight feet long. The fruit forms at the end of the branch, and has a green leafy type covering. In one variety this covering is beak shaped. In another variety, it is short and stout with a fringed end. The nut shell is thin and light brown in color.

Harvesting: If you are fortunate enough to harvest these nuts, dry them by spreading the nuts out in a dry area, and stir occasionally. To remove the inner skin after shelling, spread nuts on a baking pan and bake at about 300 F. for 15 minutes. Let the nuts cool slightly, then rub the skins off with a towel or your fingers. Chop these morsels after toasting and store in an airtight container.

Uses: Use hazelnuts as you would any other nuts. They are especially good in chocolate dishes.

Juneberry

Blueberry lovers have been know to abandon the blueberry field in search of this tasty berry.

Habitat: These small trees or shrubs can be found throughout the Northwoods. They prefer moist soils especially along a forest edge or in an open wet meadow.

Characteristics: Also called "serviceberry", the fruit ranges in color from red to deep purple and looks very much like a blueberry in shape, though a little larger. Unlike the blueberry, juneberries have soft chewable seeds.

Harvesting: They are harvested when the berries turn a dark red-purple. Store, unwashed in the refrigerator. Or freeze by spreading clean dry berries in a single layer on a cookie sheet. Freeze, then place in freezer containers and keep frozen until used.

Uses: If we are fortunate enough to beat the birds to these berries, juneberries are used in recipes just as we would use blueberries - jams, sauces, preserves, syrups, pies, and cobblers. The seeds may add an almond-like flavor when the berries are cooked.

Jerusalem Artichoke

Jerusalem artichokes are not artichokes at all, but a tall perennial sunflower.

Habitat: This plant can be found along streams, ditches, roads, and in fields where the soil is damp.

Characteristics: They can be identified by the lovely sunflower-like blossom growing on a long stem, usually three to four feet high. The flowers are smaller then sunflowers and do not have the dark centers.

Harvesting: Unlike other sunflowers, you gather the nutritious tubers. This is done in late fall, after the first frost.

Uses: Use the tubers as you would a potato; wash, peel, boil in water, and serve. Or the crunchy taste of the raw tuber lends itself well to be used in salads and main dishes, served alone as a vegetable dish, or added to sauces, soups, or stews. Jerusalem Artichokes are marketed in some parts of the country under the name "Sunchokes", and can be purchased in most supermarkets and specialty shops.

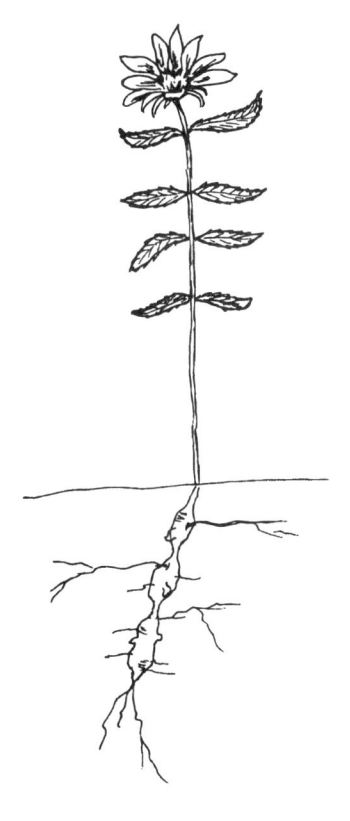

Lamb's Quarter

A relative of spinach, but more delicate in taste, this is my favorite of all the wild greens available. Lamb's Quarter is rich in calcium and Vitamin A, and contains significant amounts of thiamine, riboflavin, and niacin.

Habitat: It prefers areas where the soil has been tilled or disturbed such as fields, ditches, or along roads.

Characteristics: This plant is identified by its jagged-edged, diamond-shaped, deep green leaves. The leaves are a light dusty green on the underside.

Harvesting: The leaves of this plant can be harvested from early spring through late summer. Seeds are also gathered in late summer.

Uses: The young plants and leaves are usually prepared as cooked greens, however, they can also be used raw in salads. The seeds are wonderful in salads, main dishes, and soups, or can be added to flour to make breads.

Maple Syrup

The top maple syrup producing states are Wisconsin and Vermont. Besides tasting so good, it is a natural food and important source of energy. All varieties of maple trees produce sap high in sugar, however it is the sugar maple that produces the most syrup per gallon of sap.

Habitat: Maple trees can grow along the banks of streams, in rich well drained soils as well as on rocky hills and mountains. They prefer cooler climates.

Characteristics: Maples reach heights over 60 feet. They are best identified by the shape of their leaves.

Harvesting: Mature sugar maple trees are tapped in the early spring as soon as the sap begins to rise in the trees. A hole is drilled through the bark at an slight upward angle and a tap is snugly fitted into the hole. A sack or covered bucket is attached to catch the drips. Ideal weather for tapping is when the days are warm with freezing temperatures during the night. The sap is boiled until it forms a thick syrup. If sap is boiled too long, maple sugar will crystallize out of the syrup. It is not advisable to boil sap in the house as the dissolved sugar in the steam will make walls and cabinets sticky. Depending on the type of maple tree, it takes from 25 to 40 gallons of sap to make one gallon of syrup.

Uses: The sweet, delicate tasting syrup is perfect on pancakes, muffins, and on or in dozens of other baked goods. It can also be added to many recipes in place of sugar.

Mint

Two of the mints we know in the wild are peppermint and spearmint. Not only are these plants very aromatic but they are also rich in Vitamins A and C.

Habitat: This hardy perennial grows wild and is very easy to cultivate. It does well in sandy damp soils. If grown in your garden, it needs to be divided regularly.

Characteristics: Known for their square stems, these plants grow from one to two feet tall with leaves directly off the main stalk. When the leaves are crushed, they give off the familiar "minty" scent.

Harvesting: To use fresh, cut off tips of plant and crush leaves. Or dry, crush, and store in an airtight container.

Uses: Mint leaves are commonly used as a garnish for salads, beverages and desserts. Mint tea is soothing and welcomed any time of the year. Because the mint oil is very volatile, steep the leaves for tea instead of boiling. Bring a potted mint plant indoors to have fresh mint year-round.

Raspberries

Raspberries and blackberries are in the same family as the rose. Both berries are rich in Vitamin C and low in fat. One of the main differences between these two plants are the thorns. Because raspberries lack the hard, sharp thorns of the blackberry, they are more enjoyable to gather.

Habitat: This berry grows on large bushes which are usually 2 to 5 feet tall in open areas with moist soils. Bushes can be found growing in clumps or scattered over a large area. They can be found in many of the same places as blackberries.

Characteristics: The flower is white with 5 petals which appear from May to July. Berries will ripen to a deep red and will be ready to harvest from July to September.

Harvesting: Pick these berries when they turn a lovely deep pink-red, usually mid to late July. This delicate, highly perishable fruit should be stored unwashed in the refrigerator and used as soon as possible. The best time to harvest the leaves is in the spring, just before the flowers mature.

Use: Excellent served with cream, these berries are also great when used in sauces, jams, and preserves. As with the other berries mentioned, the leaves of this plant are valuable when used for tea. According to some herbalists, this tea is especially beneficial to women. However, this plant is best known for it's delicious red berries.

Wild Rice

This was one of the main foods of the indigenous people of North America. Not a true rice but a purple-black grain, wild rice is an excellent source of Vitamin B and high quality protein.

Habitat: Wild rice grows in shallow sections of lakes and rivers where the bottom is soft and silty and water flows slowly.

Characteristic: The plants are slender stalks with broom-like tops. They may extend about three to four feet above the water surface. The grain heads are located just below the top. The plants look very much like wheat.

Harvesting: Harvesting of wild rice is regulated in many areas. When the season is opened, people push their boat or canoe through the plants gently pulling the stalks over the boat, then lightly tapping the heads of grain with a stick. Once the rice is gathered, it is dried and processed to remove the outer husk. It is important to dry this grain completely. Wild rice is available at supermarkets or specialty shops.

Uses: The grain is low in fat and has a smoky sweet taste. It is boiled for 45 to 50 minutes in water until it swells open. If you want a crisper rice, do not boil as long. One pound of wild rice provides 20 one-half cup servings.

Wild Rose

One of my favorite wild foods, this plant offers the use of its leaves, flower petals, and fruit called rose hips (formed after the flowers have bloomed).

Habitat: These shrubs can be found along roadsides, fence lines, and streams, as well as in open fields and woods. They form thickets which can make it difficult to harvest without getting scratched.

Characteristics: The wild rose variety has many of the same features of the domestic types, including flowers ranging from white to red, and thorny branches.

Harvesting: Leaves should be harvested in the spring before the plant blossoms. Petals should be pick at the peak of their color. Store fresh leaves and petals in the refrigerator. If petals and leaves are dried, store in airtight container, preferably in a cool, dry place. The hips remain on the bushes throughout the winter, but should be harvested when fully matured, in late fall. Rose hips provide a mellow, nutlike taste and are high in Vitamin C.

Uses: The leaves, hips, and petals provide a refreshing tea, while the petals and hips can be transformed into salads, syrups, teas, jams, and sauces. The petals provide a lovely garnish to cakes and desserts and can be candied for added elegance. The dried petals are also useful as fragrant addition to potpourris. Generally, the lighter the color of the petal, the more delicate the flavor.

Wild Strawberry

A story is told that the strawberry got its name in early times when children strung the pretty red fruit on grasslike straws, calling them strawberries. This sweet, luscious berry is probably the most popular berry in America.

Habitat: Much smaller than the domestic strawberry, wild strawberries are found in open woods and clearings, on exposed slopes, and along roadsides throughout the Northwoods.

Characteristics: Wild strawberries are members of the rose family. The plants produce a 5 petaled white flower in spring which in turn produces the tasty red (sometimes white) berry, usually in late May to early July.

Harvesting: These berries should be harvested when they turn a deep red. They should be gently twisted, not pulled off the stem. Never wash fresh berries or remove the caps until just before using. Washing berries removes the natural protective outer layer, allowing them to spoil easily and lose their fresh flavor. Store berries in the refrigerator.

Use: Wild strawberries are used in all the same ways as domestic strawberries - jams, jellies, syrups, preserves, breads, pies, and desserts.

The leaves of this dainty plant are wonderful when dried and used for tea. The berry is a terrific source of Vitamin C along with B vitamins, calcium and iron.

Chapter 2
Appetizers

Berry Good
Frosty Blue Ice
Cranberry Ham Spread
Saucy Relish
Zesty Cranberry Dip
Creamy Green Dip
Crispy Green Crackers
Wild Rice Balls
Northwoods Snack Slices
Summer Taste Treats
TLC Roll Ups
Raspberry Orange
Toast Triangles
Fruit Appetizer
Zesty Fruit Dip
Bread Pudding Squares
Lemon Mint Sauce
Terra's Tea Crescents

Interesting and usually easy to prepare, these snacks and appetizers fit well into our Northwoods way of life.

Berry Good

The best snack we can think of is a bowl of fresh picked, luscious, ripe wild berries. Enjoy and savor the taste of the Northwoods.

TIP: For children, scoop these wild berries into ice cream cones for a special carry-along treat.

Frosty Blue Ice

Serve these delicious blue treats on warm summer days or deep in the heart of winter, reminding us of those summer day.

2 1/2 cups fresh wild blueberries
3 Tbsp. powdered sugar
1/4 tsp. vanilla
1 1/4 cup vanilla yogurt

Combine blueberries, sugar, and vanilla in your blender; process until well blended. Gently stir in yogurt. Spoon into ice cube trays or small paper cups. Freeze for 15 minutes, then insert a wooden stick in each cube. Freeze 4 hours, or until firm.

Cranberry Ham Spread

This mouth-watering appetizer will take top billing at your next party.

4½ oz. can deviled ham
¼ cup finely chopped, dried sweetened cranberries
1 Tbsp. sour cream
6-8 large stuffed green olives, finely chopped
6-8 large black olives, pitted and finely chopped
crushed mint leaves

Combine first five ingredients, chill well. Sprinkle with crushed mint leaves and serve on crisp crackers or with fresh vegetables, cut into serving pieces.

TIP: Substitute raisins if dried sweetened cranberries are not available.

Saucy Relish

1½ cups homemade cranberry sauce
or 1 8-oz. can commercially prepared cranberry sauce
¼ cup drained, crushed pineapple
1 Tbsp. fresh lemon juice
1 Tbsp. fresh orange juice
¼ cup chopped hazelnuts

Thoroughly combine all ingredients and chill. Serve as a side dish or as a topping for crackers. Makes about 2 cups relish.

TIP: One lemon yields about ¼ cup juice; one orange yields about ⅓ cup juice.

Zesty Cranberry Dip

A refreshing way to greet guests

    1 cup sour cream
    1/2 cup cream cheese
    1/2 cup finely chopped dried sweetened cranberries
    1 tsp. horseradish

Combine all ingredients. Chill well. Serve with fresh vegetables or crackers.

Creamy Green Dip

Serve with assorted vegetables or on Crispy Green Crackers.

    2 cups freshly gathered wild greens or spinach, finely chopped
    1 cup sour cream or plain yogurt
    1 cup cream cheese, room temperature
    1/2 cup parsley, minced
    1/2 cup green onions, chopped
    1 tsp. dill weed
    1 Tbsp. lemon juice

Combine all ingredients, blending well. Chill thoroughly. Serve with assorted vegetables.

TIP: Wild greens are wonderful in this dip, but any assortment of fresh greens will work well.

Crispy Green Crackers

Serve with cranberry spread for a colorful treat.

2 cups whole wheat flour
½ tsp. salt
½ cup sesame seeds
1 cup fresh wild greens or fresh spinach, finely minced
¼ cup oil
¾ cup cold water

Combine flour, salt, and sesame seeds. Add greens, oil and water, blending well. Roll out onto a lightly floured board until dough is very thin. Cut into squares or diamond shapes and prick with a fork. Bake at 400° F. for about 15 minutes, or until lightly browned. Cool and store in an airtight container.

Wild Rice Balls

1 egg
2 cups cooked wild rice
4 Tbsp. stale bread crumbs
2 Tbsp. minced fresh parsley
¼ cup minced green onion
Salt and pepper to taste
2 Tbsp. Italian Seasoning

Beat egg; add rice, bread crumbs, parsley, onion, and seasonings. Form into 12 to 14 small balls. Chill well. Just before serving, place on a cookie sheet and bake at 375° F. for 30 minutes. Serve warm. Makes approximately 12 appetizers.

Northwoods Snack Slices

Always a favorite. The cranberries give this snack a special zest.

> $^1/_2$ cup chopped dried sweetened cranberries
> $^1/_8$ cup finely chopped celery
> $^1/_2$ cup shredded carrots
> $^1/_2$ cup sour cream
>   Salt and pepper to taste
>   2 Tbsp. poppy seeds
>   Thinly sliced bread

Combine first six ingredients. Spread on thin slices of bread and serve as snack or appetizer.

Summer Taste Treats

Homemade — in no time!

>   2 cups chopped fresh lamb's-quarter or other fresh greens
>   1 bunch green onions, chopped
> $^1/_8$ cup cream cheese
> $^1/_8$ cup sour cream
> $^1/_2$ tsp. seasoned vinegar (such as tarragon)
>   Salt and pepper to taste

Combine all ingredients; form into balls and refrigerate. Serves 10.

TIP: When serving hors d'oeuvres on a silver tray, cover the tray with a layer of greens to protect it from the acid in the food.

TLC Roll Ups
(Turkey, lettuce and cranberry)

Easy and unusual, these rolls are a hit on any occasion.

1 lb. smoked turkey slices
Cream cheese
Cranberry sauce
Lettuce or assorted wild greens

Spread cream cheese over turkey slices, add a layer of cranberry sauce and a layer of greens. Roll up tightly and cut into serving slices. Arrange on a platter.

Raspberry-Orange Toast Triangles

Children love these unusual sweet treats.

4 slices stale bread
1/2 cup melted butter
1/2 cup brown sugar
1/2 tsp. vanilla
1/8 cup grated orange rind
1/8 cup raspberries, mashed with 1 Tbsp. sugar

Combine the brown sugar, vanilla and orange rind. Cut stale bread into triangles. Remove crusts. In oven, toast one side, brush the other side with melted butter and sprinkle with combination of brown sugar mixture and 2 tablespoons raspberry/sugar mixture. Toast in the broiler until the mixture bubbles. Serve hot. Makes 4 servings.

Fruit Appetizer

A refreshing taste treat for a hot summer days.

    2 cups fresh orange juice
    1 cup fresh lemon juice
    2 1/2 cups can crushed pineapple (in juice)
    4 cups fresh mixed wild berries
    2 cups banana slices
    3/4 cup sugar
    Mint leaves for garnish

Mix all ingredients except mint in large glass bowl and freeze. Let thaw 2 1/2 hours before serving. Serve while still frosty, garnished with sprigs of mint. Makes 12 servings.

Zesty Fruit Dip

    1 cup yogurt
    1 tsp. vanilla
    1/2 cup cranberry relish (See page 117 for recipe)
    1/4 tsp. ground nutmeg
    1/4 tsp. ground ginger
    Fruit for dipping

Combine yogurt, vanilla, relish and spices. Serve with chunks of banana, apple, pineapple, or orange slices. Makes 1 1/2 cups dip.

TIP: For the best buy in yogurt, make sure the label says "active yogurt cultures" or "living yogurt cultures" or "contains active cultures".

Bread Pudding Squares

This tasty appetizer doubles as dessert with the addition of a tangy lemon sauce.

> **8 slices stale bread**
> **½ cup sugar**
> **1 tsp. cinnamon**
> **½ tsp. nutmeg**
> **2 eggs**
> **1 cup milk**
> **1 tsp. vanilla**
> **½ cup dried sweetened cranberries**

Break bread into pieces and place in large bowl. Add remaining ingredients and stir well. Place in greased baking dish. Bake at 325° F. for 40 to 60 minutes until top is lightly browned. Cut into 1-inch squares to serve. May also be served as a dessert with **Lemon Mint Sauce** (below).

Lemon Mint Sauce

> **2 Tbsp. cornstarch**
> **3 Tbsp. sugar**
> **½ cup mint tea** (See page 31 for recipe)
> **⅓ cup light corn syrup**
> **1 Tbsp. grated lemon rind**
> **Juice of 2 lemons**

Combine sugar and cornstarch in a saucepan. Add tea and corn syrup. Cook for 5 minutes, stirring constantly. Remove from heat, add lemon juice and rind. Makes about 1 cup sauce.

Terra's Tea Crescents

Serve these tasty tidbits filled with fresh, sweet berries as a cookie or sweet roll, or filled with a savory spice mixture as an hors d' oeuvre.

2/3 cup sugar
1 cup fresh wild strawberries
3 cups flour
1/2 lb. butter
1/4 tsp. vanilla
3 well-beaten egg yolks (reserve egg whites for glaze)
1 Tbsp. yeast
8 Tbsp. buttermilk
Powdered sugar

Combine strawberries and sugar in saucepan. Crush berries and cook over medium-low heat until the mixture is reduced, about 10 minutes. Set aside.

With pastry blender, combine flour and butter until crumbly. Blend in vanilla and egg yolks. Add yeast to buttermilk, blending well to dissolve. Add to the flour mixture, blending only enough to combine. Divide mixture into 4 sections.

On a lightly floured surface, roll each section into a circle about 1/4 inch thick. Spread strawberry mixture over the top. Cut each circle into 16 wedges and roll up, starting from the wide outside end. Place on a greased cookie sheet. Brush tops with beaten egg white. Bake at 350° F. for 25 minutes. Remove from oven, cool and roll in powdered sugar. Makes about 5 dozen rolls, depending on size.

Chapter 3
Beverages

Cranberry Mint Punch
Minty Hot Chocolate
Maple Mint Sodas
Mulled Warm-Up Tea
Hot Spiced Blackberry Tea
Very Northwoods Tea
Hot Spiced Wine
Holiday Punch
Lemons and Berries
Raspberry Citrus Cooler
Chilled Rose Hip Cooler
Strawberry Cream

Each season in the Northwoods offers us an opportunity to use the foods that nature provides. Fragrant flowers, leaves, and berries provide the basis for a variety of beverages.

Cranberry Mint Punch

Float a ring of frozen cranberries in this punch as a lovely garnish. Simply thread cranberries on string or thread, tie into a ring and freeze.

- 2 cups mint tea (See page 31 for recipe)
- 1 cup sugar
- 1/4 cup cinnamon candies
- 12 whole cloves
- Four 2-inch cinnamon sticks
- 5 cups cranberry juice, chilled
- 6 oz. can frozen lemonade concentrate
- 6 oz. can frozen orange juice concentrate

Combine tea, sugar, candy, and spices and bring to a boil; simmer for about 5 minutes. Cool and remove spices. Combine with cranberry juice, lemonade concentrate, and orange juice concentrate. Pour over ice. Add a ring of frozen cranberries, and serve immediately. Makes 10 servings.

Minty Hot Chocolate

Kids, even grown-up ones, really go for this steamy beverage.

1/4 cup cocoa powder
1/2 cup sugar
1/3 cup hot strong mint tea (See page 31 for recipe)
4 cups milk
1 tsp. vanilla
whipped cream

Combine cocoa and sugar in a saucepan. Blend in tea. Bring to a boil over medium heat, stirring constantly. Reduce heat, add milk and vanilla. Stir and simmer for an additional 5 minutes, (*do not boil*). Pour into heated mugs and top with a dollop of whipped cream. Serves 6.

Maple Mint Sodas

2 1/2 qt. hot Very Northwoods Tea (See page 31 for recipes.)
1/3 cup maple syrup
3 fresh lemons, cut into wedges
6 mint sprigs
1 qt. chilled gingerale
Additional lemon slices & fresh mint for garnish

Prepare tea. Add maple syrup; stir to dissolve. Squeeze lemons and add juice to the tea, drop in squeezed lemon rinds. Add mint. Let the mixture cool, then strain. Add gingerale. Serve over lots of chipped ice, with lemon slices and mint leaves for garnish. Makes 3 1/2 quarts or 14 8-oz. servings.

Mulled Warm-Up Tea

6 oz. can frozen orange juice concentrate
2 cups cranberry juice
Two 2-inch cinnamon sticks
2 cups Very Northwoods Tea
Orange slices for garnish

Combine all ingredients except orange slices. Simmer, uncovered, for 10 minutes. *Do not boil.* Serve in warmed mugs with orange slices for garnish. Serves 12.

Hot Spiced Blackberry Tea

3 cups hot mint tea (See page 31 for recipe)
1 cup fresh lemon juice
$1/2$ cup sugar
3 cups spiced blackberry syrup (See page 112 for recipe)
Whole cloves
Cinnamon sticks
Lemon slices

Combine the first four ingredients. Add more sugar to sweeten, if necessary. Pour into mugs and serve each with lemon slice studded with cloves and a cinnamon stick. Serves 6-8.

Very Northwoods Tea

Clover, wild rose, mint, blueberry, raspberry, strawberry, or blackberry tea

Gather tender young leaves and blossoms. Dry at room temperature or in oven at very low temperature. Crush gently when dry. Seal securely in plastic bags to retain freshness. Tea leaves will stay fresh several months but they don't improve with long aging, so date each package. To test freshness, rub a bit of the leaves between your palms and breathe in the aroma. If there is no aroma, it's time to replace with fresh, fragrant leaves.

Use 1 teaspoon crushed leaves for each cup of boiling water. One tablespoon dry leaves equals 2 tablespoons fresh leaves. Brew by place leaves in a cup or teapot, add boiling water, and let stand for about 5 minutes. Strain and sweeten to taste with honey or maple syrup.

Hot Spiced Wine

One 2-inch cinnamon stick
$1/_2$ tsp. nutmeg
4 cloves
4 cups red wine
1 Tbsp. grated lemon peel
2 cups Very Northwoods Tea
$1/_2$ tsp. allspice
$1/_2$ tsp. ground ginger

Tie spices and lemon peel in a piece of cheesecloth. In a medium saucepan, combine wine and spice bag. Simmer for about 10 minutes, but do not boil. Discard spice bag. Add tea and simmer until heated through. Serves 6.

Holiday Punch

Festive and colorful, this punch is a hit no matter what the season.

2 quarts ginger ale
2 quarts spiced strawberry berry syrup (See page 112 for recipe)
1 qt. lime sherbet
2 cups fresh wild strawberries
Berries for garnish

A few hours before serving arrange strawberries evenly in a ring mold. Add sherbet to fill; refreeze until solid. Chill the punch bowl.

When ready to serve, remove the sherbet/fruit ring from the mold and place in the chilled bowl. Add ginger ale and juice slowly. Using a small fruit scoop, dot the surface of the punch with the remaining sherbet. This punch is very pretty and is a taste treat to any holiday meal. Serves 12.

TIP: Put a few sprigs of fresh mint in each cube section of an ice cube tray. Fill with clear tea or water. Freeze. Add these cubes to refreshing summer drinks for extra taste and appeal.

Lemons and Berries

¼ cup blackberries
4 cups fresh lemonade
Sugar to taste

Pureé berries in a blender; strain. Add lemonade and sweeten to taste. Serve over crushed ice, garnished with twists of lemon.

Raspberry Citrus Cooler

2 cups orange juice
2 cups lemonade
1 cup lemon sherbert
1 cup orange sherbet
Fresh wild raspberries
Mint leaves

Combine orange juice and lemonade. Pour into chilled glasses. Top with small scoops of orange and lemon sherbet. Garnish with raspberries and mint. Serve at once. Makes 4 to 6 servings.

TIP: Always chill juices and sodas before adding to recipes.

Chilled Rose Hip Cooler

$1/8$ cup rose hip syrup (See page 112 for recipe)
12 oz water
Crushed ice
Orange slices

Combine syrup and water; mix well. Pour over chipped ice. Garnish with thinly sliced orange slices. Makes 1 large glass.

Note: Roses are from the same family as strawberries, apples, cherries and plums, and are high in Vitamin C. Dried rose hips are available at many health food stores and specialty shops.

Strawberry Cream

This tasty drink can double as a light breakfast or lunch.

- 1 small banana
- 1 cup yogurt
- $1/2$ tsp. vanilla
- $3/4$ cup fresh wild strawberries, crushed
- $1/2$ cup milk
- Cinnamon

Combine banana, yogurt, vanilla, wild strawberries, and milk in blender container; process until smooth. Pour into 2 tall serving glasses and sprinkle with cinnamon. Serve immediately. Makes 2 servings.

TIP: Store glasses in freezer 30 minutes before serving to give the drinks a nice frosty look.

Chapter 4
Breads

Homemade French Bread
Holiday Bread
Homemade Croutons
Blueberry Pancakes
Southern Cornbread Goes North
Biscuits and Strawberry Butter
Fry Bread
Honey Butter
Double Cranberry Tea Bread
Mapley French Toast
Tasty Wheat Muffins
Blueberry Muffins
Hot Scones with
Blueberry Sauce
Clover Blossom Fritters
Quick Minty Muffins
Lemon-Hazelnut Scones
with Lemon Curd
Maple Gingerbread

A variety of breads compliment our meal enjoyment. Explore the aroma and taste of freshly baked breads. Share them with family and friends.

Homemade French Bread

½ cup warm water
1½ tsp. yeast
1 tsp. sugar
4 cups flour (approximate)
1 tsp. salt
1½ tsp. shortening
1 cup warm water (approximate)
¼ cup cornmeal

In a small bowl, combine water, yeast, and sugar. Let sit 10 minutes to *proof. In a large bowl, combine flour, salt, and shortening. Blend in yeast mixture, continue adding additional water (a little at a time) until dough is workable. Knead 10 minutes.

Oil a large bowl and set dough inside. Cover with a damp cloth and let rise 1½ hours. Punch down, then form into a long cylinder. Sprinkle cornmeal on a greased baking sheet. Place loaf on sheet, cover, place in warm area and let rise an additional hour. Place in 400° F. oven then spray bread with water and bake 15 minutes. Spray with water again, reduce heat to 350° F. and bake an additional 30 minutes. Cool on a wire rack. Makes 1 long loaf.

*"Proofing" is an excellent way to prepare all yeast breads. Placing water, yeast, and sugar in a bowl, stir to dissolve. Letting it sit for about 10 minutes.

Holiday Bread

2 pkg. dry yeast
$1/2$ cups warm water
3 cups milk, scalded
$1/4$ cup butter
$3/4$ cup sugar
1 cup whole wheat flour
6 to 7 cups flour
$1/2$ tsp. salt
2 eggs, beaten
1 Tbsp. orange zest
1 cup sweetened dried cranberries
1 tsp. allspice
2 Tbsp. cranberry juice
$1/4$ to $1/2$ cup powdered sugar

Dissolve yeast in $1/2$ cup lukewarm water; set aside. In a separate bowl, pour scalded milk over butter in a large bowl and stir. When this mixture is lukewarm, add yeast and sugar. Add half of the flour and salt. Beat well for 10 minutes. Add eggs and beat thoroughly. Add orange zest, cranberries, allspice, and remaining flour. Turn out onto a floured board and knead. Place dough in a greased bowl. Cover and set in a warm place until doubled in bulk.

Punch down and knead again. Divide dough into thirds. Shape into loaves and place in greased bread pans. Brush tops of loaves with beaten egg white. When again double in bulk, bake in 350° F. oven for 35 to 40 minutes. Remove from oven, brush with a mixture of cranberry juice and powdered sugar. Cool on a wire rack. Makes 3 loaves.

TIP: Frost with cranberry icing and decorate with wintergreen leaves for a wonderful holiday gift.

Homemade Croutons

Stale French bread, cut into cubes
¼ cup butter
2 cloves garlic, minced

In a skillet, melt butter and sauté garlic. Reduce heat, add bread cubes, stirring well to coat with butter. Remove the bread cubes from the skillet and place in a baking pan. Bake in a 350° F. oven, stirring occasionally, for 25 to 30 minutes, or until lightly browned.

Blueberry Pancakes

This is a wonderful Saturday morning treat served with warm maple syrup.

1 egg
1½ cups buttermilk
1 tsp. baking soda
2 cups flour
2 tsp. baking powder
1 tsp. sugar
4 Tbsp. butter, melted
1 cup fresh blueberries

In a large bowl, combine buttermilk and eggs; beat well. Add melted butter. In a separate bowl, combine baking soda, flour, baking powder, and sugar. Add dry ingredients to egg and milk mixture, blending well. Fold in blueberries. Heat a lightly oiled skillet. Drop pancake batter onto hot skillet (approx. ⅛ cup per pancake). Fry until lightly browned on each side. Makes 6 servings.

Southern Cornbread Goes North

Our family enjoys cornbread with almost any meal. Any leftovers are saved for a late night snack. Sprinkle with a little sugar over the top and pour milk or cream over that.

2 cups cornmeal
1 cup flour
2 tsp. baking soda
1/8 tsp. salt
1/4 cup butter, melted
1 egg
1/4 cup pure maple syrup
2 cups milk

Combine cornmeal, flour, baking soda and salt in bowl. In a separate bowl, combine melted butter, egg, maple syrup and milk; blend well. Gradually add cornmeal mixture to liquids. Stir just to moisten. Place in a 9-inch greased baking pan. Bake at 350° F. for approximately 35 to 40 minutes. Cut into thick wedges and serve hot with butter or berry sauce. Serves 6.

TIP: 1/3 cup crumbled bacon pieces added to the cornbread batter just before baking will give an added crunch and extra flavor to the bread.

Biscuits and Strawberry Butter

A good basic biscuit to combine with summer berries — or, omit sugar and serve with soups or stews.

>4 cups flour
>2 Tbsp. baking powder
>1 tsp. baking soda
>1/8 tsp. salt
>1 tsp. sugar
>8 tsp. butter or shortening
>1 1/2 cup buttermilk
>**Wild strawberry Butter** (recipe follows)

Combine flour, baking powder, baking soda, salt, and sugar in a bowl. Cut in butter or shortening until mixture resembles coarse meal. Stir in buttermilk to make a slightly soft dough. Pat out onto a floured board and cut into circles. Place on a greased cookie sheet. Bake at 400° F. for 15 to 20 minutes. Serve hot biscuits with **Strawberry Butter**. Makes about 24 two-inch biscuits.

Strawberry Butter

>1/4 cup butter, softened
>2 Tbsp. strong mint tea
>1 cup crushed wild strawberries
>1/4 tsp. cinnamon
>1 Tbsp. powdered sugar

Combine butter and tea. Whip with electric mixer until light and fluffy. Stir in strawberries, cinnamon, and sugar. Mix well. Serve on hot breads.

Fry Bread

This recipe was given to me by a lovely lady in Lac du Flambeau, Wisconsin. The Native Americans prepare this bread often and serve it with main dishes, sometimes accompanied by honey and butter. The bread is also served with lettuce, tomatoes, black olives cheese and taco meat. It is equally delicious served plain.

3 to 3½ cups flour
1 Tbsp. baking powder
1 Tbsp. shortening or butter
1 cup milk
⅛ tsp. salt
Oil or shortening for frying

Combine flour, salt, and baking powder. Cut in butter or shortening. Add milk, and stir just to moisten dough. Pull off chunks of dough and pat gently into a flat, round disk. Heat 1 to 2 inches of oil or shortening in a heavy skillet. *(Make sure oil is very hot or the fried bread will be greasy.)* Gently place bread pieces into hot oil. Fry for about 2 minutes on each side, or until lightly browned. Remove from oil and drain on paper towels.

Honey Butter

¼ cup softened butter
⅛ cup honey

Whip butter and honey together. Serve on hot breads. Refrigerate leftovers.

Double Cranberry Tea Bread

This delicious tea bread can be baked ahead and frozen, or keep any leftovers in the refrigerator.

- 2 cups flour
- ½ cup sugar
- ½ cup brown sugar
- 1½ tsp. baking powder
- ½ tsp. baking soda
- ½ tsp. salt
- ¼ cup butter
- ¾ cup orange juice
- 1 egg, well beaten
- 1 cup fresh cranberries, cut in half
- 1 tsp. grated orange rind
- ½ cup dried sweetened cranberries

Combine flour, sugars, baking powder, baking soda, and salt. Add butter. Cut into flour mixture until mixture resembles coarse meal. In separate bowl, combine orange juice, egg, fresh cranberries, and grated orange rind. Add egg mixture to dry ingredients; stir just to moisten. Fold in dried sweetened cranberries. Place in a greased loaf pan and bake at 350° F. for 50 to 60 minutes. Remove from pan and cool on a wire rack. Makes 1 loaf.

Maple French Toast

- 2 eggs beaten
- ¼ cup pure maple syrup

1½ cups milk
1½ cups flour
1 Tbsp. baking powder
1 cup corn meal
Homemade French Bread (See page 36 for recipe)
Powdered sugar (Optional)
1 cup pure maple syrup, warmed
Fresh wild berries

Combine eggs, maple syrup and milk, mixing well. In a separate bowl, combine flour, baking powder, and corn meal. Add to egg mixture, stirring to combine. Dip thick slices of bread in batter and fry on each side until lightly browned. Drain on paper toweling. Sprinkle with powdered sugar, if desired. Serve with warm maple syrup and fresh berries. Serves 6.

Tasty Wheat Muffins

1 cup flour
½ cup whole wheat flour
2 tsp. baking powder
⅛ tsp. salt
1 beaten egg
½ cup milk
½ cup pure maple syrup
¼ cup cooking oil
1 Tbsp. finely shredded lemon peel

In a large bowl, combine first 4 ingredients; set aside. In a separate bowl, combine remaining ingredients. Add to dry ingredients and stir just until moistened. Batter will be lumpy. Fill greased muffin tins about ⅔ full. Bake at 375° F. for 20 minutes. Makes 12 muffins.

Blueberry Muffins

No Northwoods cookbook would be complete without a recipe for blueberry muffins. These are wonderful served warm, just as they are.

    1½ cups flour
    ½ cup sugar
    2 Tbsp. baking powder
    ¼ tsp. salt
    ¼ cup butter
    1 egg, beaten
    ¾ cup buttermilk
    1 cup fresh blueberries
    1 Tbsp. finely grated lemon peel
    ¼ cup sugar mixed with 1 tsp. cinnamon

Combine flour, sugar, baking powder, and salt in large bowl; set aside. In a separate bowl, combine butter, egg, and buttermilk. Add egg mixture to dry ingredients, stirring just to moisten. Gently fold in blueberries and lemon peel. Fill greased muffin tins ⅔ full and sprinkle cinnamon-sugar mixture over tops. Bake at 400° F for 20 to 25 minutes. Remove from pans and cool on wire rack. Makes 12 muffins.

TIP: A good substitute for buttermilk is sour milk. To make sour milk: add 2 Tbsp. lemon juice or vinegar to 1 cup milk.

Hot Scones with Blueberry Sauce

1 cup oatmeal
1/2 cup flour
1 tsp. baking powder
1 Tbsp. honey
3/4 cup buttermilk
6 Tbsp. butter
Melted butter
Cinnamon and sugar

Blueberry Sauce

1 cup fresh wild blueberries
4 Tbsp. **strong mint and wild rose tea** (See page 31 for recipe)
2 Tbsp. cornstarch
1 Tbsp. powdered sugar

Combine oatmeal, flour and baking powder. In a separate bowl, combine honey and buttermilk. Blend butter into dry ingredients until mixture resembles coarse meal. Stir in honey and buttermilk. Form dough into a ball. Gently pat, or roll out, to about 1/2-inch thick. Place on a lightly greased baking sheet and score into triangle shapes. Brush top of dough with melted butter, then sprinkle on cinnamon and sugar. Bake scones for 15 to 20 minutes at 350° F.

Meanwhile, combine blueberries, tea, and cornstarch in a saucepan and bring to boil. Lower heat and simmer until mixture is thickened. Let cool. Serve warm scones with blueberry mixture over top. Sprinkle with powdered sugar. Makes 12 scones.

TIP: If frozen berries are used, don't thaw before using.

Clover Blossom Fritters

1½ cups flour
¼ cup sugar
2 tsp baking powder
1 egg, beaten
⅔ cup milk
1 tsp lemon juice
1 cup clover blossoms, washed and chopped
Vegetable oil
Powdered sugar

Combine flour, sugar, and baking powder. In separate bowl, combine beaten egg, milk, and lemon juice. Add liquid mixture to flour mixture and stir to blend. Fold in clover blossoms.

Drop teaspoonfuls of mixture into hot oil, turning as they lightly brown on each side. Drain on paper toweling. Sprinkle with powdered sugar. Serve warm. Makes 24 small fritters.

Quick Minty Muffins

⅓ cup butter
½ cup sugar
2 eggs
½ cup milk
½ cup strong mint tea (See page 31 for recipe)
1 cup flour
½ cup whole wheat flour
4 tsp. baking powder
½ tsp. nutmeg

Cream sugar and butter until light and fluffy. Add eggs and beat well. In a separate bowl, combine flours, baking powder, and nutmeg. Combine milk and tea. Add dry ingredients and milk/tea mixture alternately to creamed butter and sugar. Place in lightly greased muffin tins and bake at 375° F. for 20-25 minutes. Makes 12 muffins.

Lemon-Hazelnut Scones with Lemon Curd

1 1/3 cup flour
1/4 cup brown sugar
1 Tbsp baking powder
3/4 tsp baking soda
1/8 tsp. salt
4 Tbsp butter
1 cup wheat germ
1/2 cup chopped, toasted hazelnuts
1/2 cup dried sweetened cranberries
1 Tbsp grated lemon rind
1 egg
1 cup lemon yogurt
Sugar
Lemon Curd (See page 113 for recipe)

Combine flour, sugar, baking powder, baking soda, and salt. Add butter; cut in with pastry blender. Stir in wheat germ. Add hazelnuts and cranberries. In separate bowl, combine lemon rind, egg, and yogurt. Add to flour mixture; blend just until moistened.

On greased baking pan, pat dough into large circle, about 3/4 inch thick. Score with knife into wedges. Sprinkle top with sugar. Bake at 400° F for about 15 minutes. Serve warm with **Lemon Curd**.

Maple Gingerbread

Gingerbread is a favorite in many households. This one uses yogurt to create a soft bread, and dried sweetened cranberries to give a tangy cranberry taste.

- ½ cup pure maple syrup
- ½ cup molasses
- ¼ cup melted butter
- 1 egg, beaten
- ½ cup yogurt
- 1½ cup flour
- 2 tsp. baking soda
- 1 tsp. cinnamon
- 1 tsp. ginger
- ½ tsp. allspice
- Dash salt
- ½ cup dried sweetened cranberries

Combine syrup and molasses; beat well. Blend in melted butter. Combine beaten egg and yogurt. Pour into syrup mixture, mixing well.

Combine dry ingredients and add to batter. Stir in cranberries just to moisten. Place in 9-inch greased baking pan and bake at 325° F. for 40 minutes. Serves 6.

Chapter 5
Salads

Autumn Nut and Cranberry
Salad with Olive Oil Dressing
Crunchy Wild Rice and Yogurt Salad
Gingered Green Salad
Marinated Fruit Salad
Melon and Berry Salad
Summer Fruit Salad
Raspberry-Orange Dressing
Strawberry Fruit Salad Dressing
Tabbouleh
Tangy Dandelion and Pepper Salad
Wild Rice Salad
Wilted Spring Greens
Yogurt-Brown Sugar Dressing

A fresh salad, carefully planned, gently tossed with love and consideration for color, flavor and texture can be the focal point of a memorable meal.

Autumn Nut and Cranberry Salad

An easy-to-prepare, colorful dish for those busy fall days.

> 1 tsp. butter
> 1/2 cup chopped hazelnuts, toasted
> 1/2 cup fresh cranberries, cut in half
> 1/4 cup chopped green onions
> 4 cups assorted wild greens, washed, dried and cut into strips
> 1 1/2 cups chicken, cooked and cut into strips
> Chopped hazelnuts for garnish

Olive Oil Dressing

> 3 Tbsp. olive oil
> 1 Tbsp. tarragon vinegar
> 1/4 tsp. salt
> Freshly ground black pepper

Combine dressing ingredients in a jar with a tight lid. Shake to combine, set aside. Melt butter in a small skillet, add nuts, cranberries and onions. Cook for about 5 minutes or until cranberries are soft. Place greens and chicken in a large salad bowl, add nut-cranberry mixture and dressing; toss gently. Garnished with a sprinkling of chopped nuts. Makes 6 servings.

TIP: *One of the best herbs to use with chicken is tarragon. If you don't have tarragon vinegar, soak 1 teaspoon tarragon in 1/4 cup white wine; add to chicken during cooking.*

Crunchy Wild Rice and Yogurt Salad

2 cups cold cooked wild rice
1/2 cup chopped water chestnuts
1/2 cups fresh sliced mushrooms
1/2 cup diced cucumber
1/2 cup Jerusalem Articoke, peeled and chopped
1/2 cup yogurt
1 Tbsp. herbed vinegar
1/2 tsp. salt

Combine first five ingredients in a salad bowl and mix well. In a separate bowl, combine yogurt, vinegar, and salt. Combine both mixtures and toss. Serves 6.

Gingered Green Salad

1 cup mushrooms, sliced
Large bowl of dandelion greens, washed and patted dry
1/2 cup chopped green onions
1/2 cup diced sweet red pepper
2 Tbsp. fresh lemon juice
1 Tbsp. fresh gingerroot, peeled and grated
1 tsp. soy sauce
2 Tbsp. olive oil
Garlic croutons (See page 38 for recipe)

Combine mushrooms, dandelion greens, onion, and pepper in a large bowl. Combine lemon juice, gingerroot, soy sauce, and olive oil in a jar with a tight fitting lid; shake vigorously. Pour dressing over greens and toss. Garnish with croutons. Makes 4 servings.

Marinated Fruit Salad

This sweet fruit combo serves as a salad, or — topped with whipped cream and sprinkled with nuts — a fabulous dessert.

 1 cup fresh wild blackberries
 1 cup fresh peaches, sliced
 1 cup fresh wild strawberries, halved
 1 cup fresh wild blueberries
 1 cup fresh wild raspberries
 1 large banana, sliced
 1/8 cup sugar
 2 Tbsp. blackberry brandy or blackberry syrup

Combine fruit in a large glass bowl. Add sugar and brandy/syrup. Gently stir and chill before serving. Makes 6 servings.

Melon and Berry Salad

 1 1/2 cups plain yogurt
 1/4 cup orange juice
 1 tsp. grated orange rind
 1 cup fresh wild berries
 2 cups assorted melon pieces
 Chopped Hazelnuts

Combine yogurt, orange juice, and orange rind, mix well and chill, covered until ready to use. Combine berries and melon in large bowl. When ready to serve, fold dressing gently into fruit and serve in frosty glass bowls. Garnish with a sprinkle of chopped hazelnuts.

Summer Fruit Salad

Enjoy the cool sweetness of melons, combined with the summer freshness of berries in a main dish salad. Add a full-grained bread and minty iced tea for a refreshing summer meal.

$\frac{1}{4}$ cup flavored vinegar
$\frac{1}{4}$ cup honey
1 Tbsp. light olive oil
1 tsp. lemon juice
4 cups melon balls
$\frac{1}{2}$ pound fresh wild greens
1 cup cooked chicken, cut into strips
$\frac{1}{2}$ cup fresh wild berries

Combine vinegar, honey, oil, and lemon juice in a jar with a tight fitting lid; shake vigorously. In a large bowl, combine melon balls and $\frac{1}{2}$ of the vinegar mixture. Mix gently, cover and chill. When ready to serve, tear greens into bite sized pieces; add to a large bowl along with additional vinegar mixture and chicken pieces. Mix to combine ingredients. Sprinkle berries over the top and serve. Makes 4 servings.

TIP: The finest olive oil is light in color and has a lighter taste. If you choose a darker olive oil, dilute it with salad oil to lighten the taste.

TIP: Chill berries before washing to prevent mushiness.

Raspberry-Orange Dressing

1 cup wild raspberries
1/2 cup vanilla yogurt
1 tsp. grated orange rind
1 Tbsp. orange juice

Combine first three ingredients, mix well and serve chilled over any combination of fruit or berries. Garnish with fresh wild raspberries.

Strawberry Fruit Salad Dressing

1 cup vanilla flavored yogurt
1 Tbsp. brown sugar
1/4 cup fresh strawberries, chopped
Mint leaves for garnish

Combine all ingredients, mix well and serve chilled over any combination of fruit or berries, or over pound cake for dessert. Garnish with fresh mint leaves. Makes 1 1/4 cups dressing.

Tabbouleh

1 cup fine bulgur (cracked wheat)
1 2/3 cups boiling water
2 cups chopped fresh parsley
1/3 cup finely chopped fresh mint leaves
1/2 cup fresh lemon juice
1/4 cup olive oil
1 cup finely chopped chives
1 large tomato
1 cucumber
Salt and pepper to taste

Place bulgur into a large mixing bowl, cover with boiling water and let soak for 2 hours, or until wheat has softened and water is absorbed. Combine parsley, mint, lemon juice, oil, and chives in a mixing bowl. Finely chop tomato and cucumber; add to parsley mixture. Add bulgur; season with salt and pepper to taste. Chill overnight. Serve on fresh wild greens or in pita bread. Garnish with fresh mint leaves. Serves 6.

TIP: Bulgur is a precooked, dried cracked wheat with a toasted look and a nutty flavor. It probably is man's oldest use of wheat. It can be purchased commercially or made from whole wheat.

Tangy Dandelion and Pepper Salad

    3 cups dandelion greens, washed, dried and torn into pieces
    1/2 cup sliced fresh mushrooms
    2 Tbsp. fresh chives, chopped
    1/4 tsp. salt
    1 tsp. freshly ground pepper
    1/8 cup Dijon style mustard
    1/4 cup olive oil
    2 Tbsp. red wine vinegar
    Garlic seasoned croutons
    Toasted sesame seeds

Place greens, mushrooms and chives in large bowl, toss. In a jar with a screw-type lid, combine salt, pepper, mustard, olive oil, and vinegar; shake vigorously. Pour over greens and toss gently. Garnish with garlic croutons and a sprinkle of sesame seeds. Serve immediately. Makes 6 servings.

TIP: Carefully wash tender greens; wrap in towel and store in refrigerator until ready to use. This will keep them fresh and crisp.

Wild Rice Salad

This salad is especially nice with wild game.

1/2 cup wild rice uncooked
2 1/2 cups chicken broth
1/2 cup brown rice, uncooked
1 clove garlic, minced
3/4 cup diced carrots
1/2 cup chopped celery
1/2 cup chopped green onions
1/4 cup chopped fresh parsley
1/8 cup tarragon vinegar
1 Tbsp. olive oil
1/4 tsp. salt
Freshly ground pepper
3 Tbsp. chopped hazelnuts

Rinse *wild rice in three changes of hot water; drain and set aside. Bring broth to a boil in saucepan. Stir in wild rice, brown rice, and garlic; cover and reduce heat. Simmer 40 minutes or until rice is tender. Drain and reserve broth for other use, set rice aside. Steam carrots over boiling water 3 minutes. Combine rice, carrots, celery, onions, and parsley in a bowl; set aside. Combine vinegar, oil, salt and pepper in a tightly covered jar. Shake vigorously. Pour over rice mixture and toss to blend. Sprinkle chopped hazelnuts over salad. Makes 6 servings.

* Wild rice is available in larger supermarkets or in specialty food stores.

TIP: Whenever a meat or chicken recipe calls for water, substitute broth instead. The results will be much richer tasting.

Wilted Spring Greens

Grandma served these wilted greens to her family every spring. For variety, she steamed them for about 20 minutes, and sprinkled them with crisp bacon pieces, salt, pepper, and a touch of nutmeg. When these tender dandelion greens were not available, she substituted lettuce or other greens.

1/4 cup bacon pieces (4-6 slices)
2 tsp. sugar
Salt and freshly ground pepper
3 Tbsp. vinegar
Large bowl dandelion greens, torn into bite-sized pieces

Fry bacon until crisp. Remove all but 1 tablespoon bacon fat from skillet. Add sugar, salt, pepper, and vinegar to skillet with bacon. Continue to cook for 1 minute, stirring. Pour over steamed greens and toss well to mix. Serves 6.

Yogurt-Brown Sugar Dressing

1 cup vanilla flavored yogurt
1/2 cup yogurt cheese (See page 113 for recipe)
2 Tbsp. brown sugar
1/2 tsp. cinnamon
2 Tbsp. pure maple syrup

Combine ingredients, mix well and serve over any combination of fruit or berries. Sprinkle crunchy granola, toasted oats, or crushed ginger cookies over top for garnish. Makes 1 1/2 cups dressing.

Chapter 6
Soups

Beef Stock
Chicken Stock
Bouquet Garni
Vegetable Stock
Chilled Vegetable, Bean
and Melon Soup
Double Rice Soup
Spring Soup
Raspberry and Rose Hip Soup
Blueberry Soup
Summer Strawberry Soup
Chilly Cranberry Soup
Fragrant Green Soup
Mushroom and Green
Noodle Soup
Festive Vegetable Soup

Whether rich and full bodied, or clear and delicate, homemade soup adds a warm dimension to large meals, or becomes the center of a delightful, light meal. These recipes all include freshly gathered wild foods. However, as always, feel free to substitute what is available to you. The first few recipes are presented as a starting point....stock to be used in soups, sauces, main dishes and gravies. There is no comparison between these and the commercial bouillon cubes or granules. Enjoy preparing these recipes, and remember to be creative, adding what you have on hand.

Beef Stock

4 to 5 pounds fresh beef and veal bones, cut into pieces (about 2")
2 large onions, quartered
2 large tomatoes, quartered
4 large cloves garlic, cut into pieces
2 stalks celery, cut into 2-inch pieces
2 medium carrots, cut into 2-inch pieces
Water

Preheat oven to 375° F. Place bones on a rimmed cookie sheet and roast in the oven for about 2 hours. Add remaining ingredients and roast an additional 30-45 minutes.

Remove from oven, add all ingredients to a large stockpot, scraping the cookie sheet clean. Cover with water and bring to a boil. Reduce heat, and simmer for 4 to 6 hours, adding water as necessary. Cool, strain, and store in the refrigerator to be used as a base for soups, main dishes, gravies and sauces. This stock can be kept in the refrigerator for 3 to 4 days, or in the freezer up to two months.

Chicken Stock

4 to 5 pounds fresh chicken bones
(*I use the backs, necks and wings*)
1 large onion, quartered
2 large carrots, cut into 2-inch pieces
1 stalk celery, cut into 2-inch pieces
2 cloves garlic, cut into pieces
Bouquet Garni (Recipe below)
Water

Place all ingredients in large stockpot, cover with water, and bring to a boil. Reduce heat and simmer, uncovered, for 3-4 hours, adding additional water as necessary. Remove bouquet garni. Cool, strain, and store the stock in the refrigerator to be used as a base for soups, main dishes, gravies, and sauces. Can be kept stored in the refrigerator up to 3 days, in the freezer about two months.

Bouquet Garni

4 sprigs parsley
1 whole bay leaf, crushed
$1/4$ tsp. thyme
$1/4$ tsp. rosemary
3 cloves garlic, crushed
5 peppercorns

Place all ingredients in the center of a 4" x 4" square of cheesecloth. Gather ends together and tie securely. Drop in soup or broth for seasoning.

Vegetable Stock

1 quart water
4 potatoes, cut into pieces
4 medium carrots, cut into pieces
1 large onion, quartered
4 cloves garlic, cut into pieces
lettuce or wild greens, torn into pieces

Place all ingredients into a large stockpot. Bring to a boil, cover and simmer, about 4 hours, adding additional water as necessary. Strain. Stock can be kept refrigerated up to 3 days, or in the freezer up to two months.

Chilled Vegetable, Bean and Melon Soup

2 cups garbanzo beans, cooked in chicken stock and drained
2 cups fresh Jerusalem Articokes, peeled and chopped
1/4 cup chopped sweet green pepper
1 large cucumber, chopped (reserve 1/4 cup for garnish)
1 cup cantaloupe, peeled, seeded and chopped
2 large tomatoes, peeled, seeded and chopped
1/4 cup chopped chives
2 cups tomato juice
1/4 cup chopped mint leaves
1 cup plain low-fat yogurt

In a large bowl, combine all ingredients except yogurt. Blend well. Cover and chill for 2 to 24 hours. Serve in individual soup bowls, garnished with yogurt. Serves 4.

Double Rice Soup

This hearty soup works well as a main dish with the addition of a salad and crusty Italian bread.

2 slices bacon
²/₃ cup wild rice, rinsed
¼ cup brown rice
1 small onion, diced
2 cloves garlic, minced
4 medium carrots, diced
½ cup Jerusalem artichokes, diced
5 cups beef stock
1 Tbsp. butter
1 Tbsp. flour
1½ cup milk
¼ cup fresh mushrooms, chopped
Salt and freshly ground pepper, to taste
Minced fresh parsley for garnish

Cook bacon in a skillet until crisp. Remove bacon from skillet; reserve. Add wild rice, brown rice, onion, and garlic to skillet and sauté in bacon fat. Add carrots and Jerusalem artichokes and sauté an additional 2 to 3 minutes. Drain fat. Place all these ingredients into a large stockpot, adding beef stock. Heat just until boiling. Reduce heat and simmer about 1 hour, uncovered. Stirring occasionally until rice is tender.

Combine butter and flour until smooth; stir into soup. Stir in milk and continue cooking until mixture begins to thicken. Add mushrooms and simmer 4-5 minutes. Season to taste with salt and pepper. Serve in individual bowls, garnished with parsley and crumbled bacon pieces. Makes 8 servings.

Spring Soup

2 Tbsp. olive oil
1 small onion, chopped
2 cloves garlic, minced
4 cups chicken stock
1 bay leaf
Salt and pepper, to taste
4 cups greens, finely chopped (young dandelion greens and lamb's quarter mixture)
2 strips bacon, cooked crisp and crumbled
Freshly grated Parmesan cheese

Heat olive oil in skillet. Sauté onion and garlic until transparent. Add chicken stock, bay leaf, salt and pepper to taste. Simmer 5 to 10 minutes. Add greens and cook another 3 minutes, then remove bay leaf. Serve in individual bowls with bacon pieces and a sprinkling of grated Parmesan cheese for garnish. Serves 4.

Wild Raspberry and Rose Hip Soup

2 cups wild raspberries
$1/2$ cup dried rose hips
$1/2$ cup cranberry juice
$1/2$ cup raspberry tea (See page 31 for recipe)
2 Tbsp. pure maple syrup
$1/8$ tsp. freshly grated nutmeg

In a medium saucepan, combine raspberries, rose hips, cranberry juice, tea, and maple syrup. Cook over low heat about 10 minutes. Strain and transfer to a serving bowl; chill thoroughly. Serve sprinkled with freshly grated nutmeg. Serves 4.

Blueberry Soup

This wonderful chilled soup doubles as a sauce, over ice cream or pound cake.

    2 cups wild blueberries
    2 cups cranberry juice
    1/4 cup honey
    2 Tbsp. lemon juice
    1 tsp. lemon zest
    1/4 cup lemon yogurt
    Cinnamon

Combine berries and cranberry juice in a saucepan. Bring to a boil, then reduce heat. Add honey, lemon juice, and zest. Simmer, uncovered, for about 20 minutes, stirring occasionally. Remove from heat and let cool. When cool, place in a blender container and blend well. Chill. Before serving, garnish with lemon yogurt sprinkled with a dash of cinnamon. Serves 4.

Summer Strawberry Soup

    2 cups wild strawberries
    4 cups milk
    2 Tbsp. pure maple syrup
    1/4 cup chopped hazelnuts
    1/2 tsp. cinnamon

Place strawberries in blender; add milk. Cover and blend well. (*You may have to do this in halves, so that it doesn't overflow your blender container.*) Add syrup, one tablespoon at a time; blend. Chill thoroughly. To serve, place in individual serving dishes and sprinkle with chopped hazelnuts and cinnamon. Serves 4.

Chilly Cranberry Soup

6 cups fresh cranberries
4 cups apple juice
2 whole cloves
2 whole cinnamon sticks
2 Tbsp. cornstarch
1½ cup orange juice
1 cup sugar
2¼ cups orange flavored yogurt
Lemon Curd (See page 113 for recipe) **and**
Coconut, toasted, for garnish

In saucepan, combine cranberries and apple juice with cloves and cinnamon sticks; simmer 10 minutes. Drain and reserve liquid. Discard cloves and cinnamon sticks. Place cranberries in a blender and purée. Strain, and mix in 1 cup of reserved liquid.

Combine cornstarch with ¼ cup orange juice and mix well. Set aside. In a bowl, combine sugar and yogurt with remaining orange juice. Place cranberries and sugar mixture into a large saucepan. Stir in cornstarch mixture, and cook over low heat, stirring constantly. Bring to a boil, reduce heat, and simmer 10 minutes. Refrigerate until well chilled. Serve in individual bowls, garnished with a dollop of lemon curd and a sprinkling of toasted coconut. Serves 6.

Fragrant Green Soup

1 medium carrot, peeled and chopped
1 onion, chopped
1 clove garlic, minced
1 potato, peeled and chopped

½ cup Jerusalem Articokes, peeled and chopped
3 to 4 cups chicken stock
4 to 5 cups wild greens (dandelion, lamb's quarter, spinach)
1 cup milk
⅓ cup melted butter
⅓ cup flour
2 Tbsp. lemon juice

In a saucepan, combine carrot, onion, garlic, and potato. Cover with chicken stock and cook until tender; cool. Place in blender container with greens; purée and set aside. (*You may have to do this in parts so that it doesn't overflow your blender container.*)

Meanwhile, in a small saucepan, over low heat, combine milk, 1 cup chicken stock, butter, flour, and lemon juice. Cook until thickened. Add reserved vegetable mixture. Simmer on low heat until ready to serve. Serves 4.

Mushroom and Green Noodle Soup

2 tsp. garlic, chopped
¼ cup olive oil
1 pound fresh mushrooms, sliced
   (reserve ½ cup, thinly sliced for garnish)
¼ cup loosely packed fresh mint leaves, finely chopped
2 Tbsp. fresh parsley, finely chopped
Salt and pepper, to taste
3 cups chicken stock
3 cups Green Noodles (See page 88 for recipe)
¼ cup fresh chives, chopped
¼ cup finely grated carrots

Sauté garlic in oil, then add mushrooms, mint, parsley, salt, and pepper to taste. Cook, stirring constantly for about 10 minutes. Add stock and bring to a boil. Reduce heat and simmer for 15 minutes.

Add noodles and cook an additional 15 to 20 minutes. Serve in individual bowls, garnished with chopped chives and grated carrots. Serves 4.

Festive Vegetable Soup

1/2 Tbsp. olive oil
3 medium carrots, peeled and shredded
1 cup Jerusalem artichokes, peeled and shredded
1 cup turnips, peeled and shredded
3 medium potatoes, peeled and shredded
2 cloves garlic, minced
4 cups chicken stock
1 Tbsp. tarragon flavored vinegar
1 tsp. thyme, crushed
Salt and freshly ground pepper to taste
Garlic Croutons (See page 38 for recipe) and
Freshly grated Parmesan cheese, for garnish

Heat oil in a large skillet. Add carrots, artichokes, turnips, and potatoes. Sauté until vegetables are nicely browned. Stir in garlic. Reduce heat and cook an additional 3 minutes.

Place this mixture in a large saucepan or stockpot, add chicken stock, and simmer over low heat until vegetables are tender, about 20 minutes. Add vinegar and seasonings; simmer an additional 5 minutes. Serve in individual bowls with garlic flavored croutons and a sprinkle of freshly grated Parmesan cheese. Makes 6 servings.

Chapter 7
Entrées

Grilled Chicken with Wild Rice
Chicken Fried Rice
Grandma's Chicken
and Dumplings
Wild Rice and Roasted
Chicken with Herbs
Chilled Chicken with Wild Rice
Maple Cranberry Ham Bake
Northwoods Meatballs
Individual Main Dish Pies
French Bread Sandwiches
Oven Stew
Northwoods Style Beans
n' Rice
Wild Rice and Summer
Vegetables
Savory Summer Pie
Vegetarian Chili

Hearty and filling, or lightly satisfying, these main dish recipes offer a taste of the bounty we can experience by using foods naturally available to us.

Grilled Chicken with Wild Rice

Add a salad and light fruit dessert for a healthy, satisfying meal.

- 2 cloves garlic, finely chopped
- 1 tsp. olive oil
- 2 Tbsp. tarragon vinegar
- 1/2 tsp. curry powder
- 1/4 tsp. ground cardamom
- 2 Tbsp. pineapple juice
- 1/2 tsp. soy sauce
- 1/4 tsp. salt
- 1/4 tsp. freshly ground pepper
- 3/4 lb. boneless chicken breasts, skin removed
- 1 cup wild rice
- 3 cups chicken stock

Sauté garlic in 1 teaspoon olive oil. Remove from heat and add vinegar, curry powder, cardamom, pineapple juice, soy sauce, salt, and pepper. Place in a glass bowl and add chicken breasts. Marinate chicken for about 2 hours, turning occasionally. Approximately 1 hour before serving, cook wild rice in chicken stock. Remove chicken from marinade (reserve marinade). Grill over medium-high heat, turning once, until tender. Meanwhile, simmer remaining marinade sauce. Serve chicken on top of wild rice with sauce drizzled over top. Serves 4.

Chicken Fried Rice

This stick-to-the-ribs main dish is as nutritious as it is easy to prepare.

2 Tbsp. vegetable oil
1 cup wild rice
1 cup chicken broth
1 cup water
¼ cup soy sauce
2 cups finely chopped cooked chicken
2 Tbsp. olive oil
½ cup shredded carrot
½ cup chopped green pepper
½ cup sliced green onion
1 cup fresh mushrooms, sliced
2 eggs, beaten
vegetable oil
⅛ cup lemon juice

Heat oil in skillet, add wild rice, chicken broth, water, and soy sauce. Cover and reduce heat. Simmer for 45 minutes, or until rice is tender. Meanwhile, sauté carrots, green pepper, green onion, and mushrooms in olive oil. Stir into the rice. Add the cooked chicken and lemon juice to rice mixture. Simmer over low heat about 10 minutes.

Beat 2 eggs, pour into lightly oiled skillet and cook like a flat pancake. Remove from skillet and cut into strips. Add to the rice mixture, cook additional 5 minutes. Serve immediately, with extra soy sauce if desired. Makes 6 servings.

TIP: Fresh mushrooms should be trimmed at the base of the stalk. To clean mushrooms, wipe with damp cloth or simply rinse with cold water.

Grandma's Chicken and Dumplings

Fond memories will be made with this tasty combination of chicken and dumplings.

> 1 stewing chicken, cut into pieces
> 1 small onion, chopped
> 1 clove garlic, chopped
> 2 large carrots, cut into pieces
> 4 quarts water
> 1 tsp. rosemary, crushed
> 1 bay leaf

Dumplings

> 2 cups flour
> 1 cup lamb's quarter seeds (Optional)
> 1 tsp. salt
> 1 egg, beaten
> **water or vegetable water to make stiff dough**

Place the first 7 ingredients in a large pot. Bring to a boil, then reduce heat, and simmer for 40 to 50 minutes. Remove bay leaf and chicken from broth. Bone and skin the chicken. Return the meat back to the broth and continue to simmer, covered for 20 minutes.

Meanwhile, in a bowl, combine flour, lamb's quarter seeds and salt. Make a well in the center of the dry ingredients and add egg. With a fork, begin to combine these ingredients, adding enough water to make a stiff dough. Do not handle more than is necessary.

Turn the dough onto a floured cutting board. Pat or roll dough out to about 1/4 inch thick (thinner, if you prefer a noodle-like dumpling). With a sharp knife, cut dough into strips about 1-inch wide. Cut across to make dumplings about 1 inch by 2 inches. Carefully, lower dumplings into the simmering broth, and adjust heat to medium-low. Cover and cook for about 10 minutes. Serve immediately. Makes 6 servings.

Note: Dumplings need support while cooking, so always cook in broth over meat or vegetables.

Wild Rice and Roasted Chicken with Herbs

3 lb. roasting chicken
1 large onion, sliced
¼ tsp. salt
½ tsp. marjoram
½ tsp. thyme
½ tsp. rosemary
Dash of pepper
4 cups wild rice, cooked in chicken broth

Place chicken in a baking pan. Combine seasonings and sprinkle over the chicken. Cover and bake at 375° F. for 1 hour, or until chicken is tender. Remove cover and continue to bake chicken for an additional 10 minutes. Serve with wild rice. Makes 6 servings.

Chilled Chicken and Wild Rice

4 cups cooked wild rice
1 cup plain yogurt
¼ cup mayonnaise
2 cups cooked chicken, cubed
2 cups fresh lamd's quarter, cut into strips
¼ cup chopped chives
1 medium tomato, chopped

Combine all ingredients in a large serving dish. Chill. Serve with french bread and corn on the cob for a perfect summer meal. Serves 4.

Maple Cranberry Ham Bake

1 ham slice, 1½ to 1¼ inch thick
Whole cloves
3 Tbsp. pure maple syrup
1 Tbsp. tarragon vinegar
1 cup cranberry sauce
2 Tbsp. honey mustard

Remove fat from ham slice, and slash ham at 2 to 3 inch intervals to prevent curling during cooking. Stud the meat with cloves every inch or two. Place the ham in a baking dish. Combine remaining ingredients and spread over ham slice. Bake uncovered in a 300° F. oven for 1 hour, or until meat is very tender, basting occasionally. Serves 4.

TIP: Honey mustard adds great taste to dishes containing ham, chicken, or turkey. You'll find this tangy mustard in the condiment section of most supermarkets, or in gourmet shops.

Northwoods Meatballs

Cranberry sauce gives this easy-to-prepare main dish just the right amount of tang.

- 1 lb. ground round
- 1 clove garlic, finely chopped
- 1 small onion, finely chopped
- 1 egg, beaten
- 1/2 cup seasoned bread crumbs
- 1/8 cup Parmesan cheese, grated
- 1/8 tsp. pepper
- 1/2 cup tomato sauce
- 1/2 cup beef broth (See page 60 for recipe)
- 1 cup cranberry sauce (See page 118 for recipe)
- 1 Tbsp. Worcestershire sauce

Combine meat, garlic, onion, egg, bread crumbs, cheese, and pepper in large bowl. Form into meatballs. Cook over medium heat in a heavy skillet until browned and meat is cooked through. Meanwhile, combine remaining ingredients in a saucepan and cook over medium heat for 5 minutes, stirring occasionally. Pour sauce over meatballs and simmer, covered, for 40 to 45 minutes. Serve as a main dish or prepare small meatballs and serve as an appetizer. Makes 4-5 main dish servings.

TIP: Keep a supply of cranberries in your freezer for year-round use. They do not have to be defrosted before using.

Individual Main Dish Pies

Crust

1 Tbsp. yeast
1/2 tsp. sugar
1/4 cup warm water
2 1/2 cups flour
1 tsp. salt
1 egg, beaten
1/3 cup milk
1/3 cup vegetable stock
2 Tbsp. olive oil

Filling

6 cups mixed wild greens
1/2 cup chicken broth
1 Tbsp. olive oil
1/2 cup finely chopped chives
2 Tbsp. finely chopped fresh mint leaves
2/3 cup shredded mozzarella cheese
1/3 cup chicken broth
1/4 tsp. fresh ground pepper
1 egg, beaten
1/4 cup sesame seeds

Combine yeast and sugar, and dissolve in 1/4 cup warm water. Let stand for about 10 minutes. Meanwhile, combine flour and salt in a large bowl. In a separate bowl, combine egg, milk, vegetable stock, and olive oil. Add the yeast mixture; stir to blend well. Combine flour mixture and the egg mixture until the dough is smooth. Turn out onto a lightly floured surface and knead about 5 minutes, adding flour as necessary to prevent sticking. Shape the dough into a ball, place in large oiled bowl, cover, and let rise about 45 minutes.

Meanwhile, cook the greens in chicken broth for 2 to 3 minutes. Drain and squeeze out excess moisture. Finely chop greens; set aside. In a heavy skillet, sauté chives and mint in olive oil. Stir this mixture into the fresh greens, along with the cheese, egg, chicken broth, and pepper. Set this mixture aside.

Punch down dough and knead for about 5 minutes. Pinch off pieces large enough to pat or roll out into a circle about 8 inches in diameter. Place each circle on a lightly oiled baking sheet. Spoon $1/4$ cup filling on one side of the dough circle. Moisten edges and fold dough over. Using a fork, seal and crimp around the edges. Prepare remaining pies. Brush tops with milk and sprinkle sesame seeds over each. Bake at 350° F for 30 to 35 minutes, or until pastry edges are crisp and golden brown. Serve immediately. Makes 6-8 individual main dish pies.

French Bread Sandwiches

1 large, or 2 shorter (4") loaves French bread
Fresh, tender wild greens, shredded
$1/4$ cup shredded carrots
1 cucumber, thinly sliced
$1/2$ cup chopped fresh mushrooms
1 red onion, thinly sliced
$1/2$ cup alfalfa sprouts
1 Tbsp. raspberry flavored vinegar (Purchase at specialty stores)
Freshly ground pepper
$1/4$ cup feta cheese, crumbled

Slice bread horizontally, but don't cut all the way through. Layer bread with fresh greens, vegetables, and sprouts, drizzling vinegar over all. Sprinkle with freshly ground black pepper and top with crumbled cheese. Press the top layer of the bread down, and slice into serving sizes. Add a fresh green salad and cool mint tea for a satisfying meal.

Oven Stew

2 onions, sliced
1 clove garlic, chopped
½ cup celery, cut into pieces
1 Tbsp. olive oil
1½ lb lean stew meat
1 cup carrots, cut up
2 large Jerusalem Articokes, cut into chunks
1 Tbsp. Worcestershire sauce
¼ cup dry red wine
½ cup dried sweetened cranberries
1 cup tomato juice
½ cup beef broth
1 tsp. salt

Sauté onions, garlic, and celery in olive oil. Combine remaining ingredients and place in a baking dish. Cover with tight fitting lid. (*To ensure a tight cover, arrange a piece of aluminum foil over the top of the baking dish. Place the cover of the baking dish over the aluminum foil.*) Bake for 5½ hours at 275° F. Makes 6 hearty servings.

TIP: *After trimming the end and the outer stalks of the celery which may have been damaged, remove the tough, coarse fibers before cutting into desired pieces.*

Northwoods Style Beans n' Rice

Treat yourself to the tempting taste combination of rice and beans with this easy-to-prepare main dish.

    3 cups chicken broth
    1 cup dry lentils
    1 small onion, chopped
    2 cloves garlic, finely chopped
    1 cup wild rice, partially cooked (20 minutes in chicken broth)
    1/4 cup dry vermouth
    1/4 tsp. salt
    1 Tbsp. Worcestershire Sauce
    1/4 tsp. thyme
    1/4 cup dried bread crumbs
    1/4 cup grated Parmesan cheese

Combine all ingredients except bread crumbs and cheese. Place in a baking dish, cover and bake at 350° F. for 2 hours, checking occasionally to see if more liquid is needed. Top with bread crumbs and grated Parmesan cheese. Serve immediately. Makes 4 servings.

Note: Lentils have soft outer skins and don't require lengthy soaking times before cooking.

Wild Rice and Summer Vegetables

2 cups wild rice, cooked in 6 cups chicken broth
¼ tsp. salt
1 medium carrot, cut into pieces
1 clove garlic, finely chopped
2 stalks celery, chopped
1 small zucchini, cut into pieces
¾ cup broccoli cut into bite-sized pieces
1 cup sliced fresh mushrooms
1 cup chicken broth
1 cup fresh pea pods
1 Tbsp. fresh lemon juice
1 cup mild cheese, grated (such as cheddar or farmer's cheese)

Rinse rice and cook in broth for about 40 minutes. Meanwhile, prepare vegetables. Combine wild rice with the remaining ingredients, except cheese. Place in a baking dish, cover, and bake in a 375° oven about 30 minutes. Sprinkle cheese over top and bake, uncovered, for an additional 5 minutes. Serve immediately. Makes 5 servings.

TIP: To peel garlic easily, place a clove of garlic on a cutting board. Press with the flat edge of a large knife blade. The clove of garlic will easily pop out of the skin.

Savory Summer Pie

Here's what the enjoyment of summer eating is all about.

4 Tbsp. olive oil
3 cups thinly sliced unpeeled zucchini
1 cup assorted wild greens, finely chopped
2 cloves garlic, finely chopped
2 medium onions, chopped
$\frac{1}{2}$ cup chopped fresh parsley
$\frac{1}{2}$ tsp. salt
$\frac{1}{2}$ tsp. pepper
$\frac{1}{2}$ tsp. marjoram
2 eggs, slightly beaten
2 tsp. Dijon-style mustard
Dash of tabasco sauce
$1\frac{1}{2}$ cups shredded Mozzarella cheese
$\frac{1}{4}$ cup grated Parmesan cheese
Prepared pie dough

Heat olive oil in a large saucepan over medium low heat. Add zucchini, greens, garlic, and onion. Sauté until tender, about 5 minutes. Stir in parsley, salt, pepper, and marjoram; remove from heat. Combine eggs, mustard, tabasco, and cheeses in a large bowl. Add the vegetable mixture, stirring to blend. Prepare the pie dough, roll out, and place in a 10-inch pie pan. Add the vegetable/cheese filling. Bake in a preheated moderate oven (375° F.) for 35 to 40 minutes, or until a knife inserted into the pie comes out clean. Let stand 10 minutes. Makes 6 servings.

Note: Fresh parsley is available in two varieties: curly and Italian (which is flat leaved). Either variety is an excellent garnish and provides a pleasant taste to many dishes.

Vegetarian Chili

Beans and wild rice team up to provide a filling, nutritious main dish.

  2 cups chicken broth
  1 1/2 cups tomato juice
  1 cup wild rice
  1 cup partially cooked mixed beans
  1 large green pepper, seeded and chopped
  1 large onion, chopped
  2 cloves garlic, finely chopped
  2 Tbsp. olive oil
  2 Tbsp. fresh parsley, finely chopped
  2 Tbsp. soy sauce
  2 Tbsp. chili powder
  2 tsp. ground cumin
  2 Tbsp. honey
  1/4 cup shredded cheddar cheese

Place broth, tomato juice, wild rice, and beans in a large saucepan. Heat to boiling, then reduce heat. Simmer for 40 to 45 minutes.

Add the chopped pepper to cooked rice and beans. Sauté garlic and onions in olive oil and add to the rice/bean mixture. Add the parsley, soy sauce, chili powder, cumin, and honey. Simmer over low heat for about 5 minutes.

Cover and place in a 400° oven for 35 to 40 minutes. Stir and serve hot, garnished with shredded cheese. Makes 6 servings.

Chapter 8
Vegetables

Country Style Lamb's Quarter
Cranberry Spiced Squash
Carrots in Mint Tea
Maple Mint Yams
Spiced Sweet Potatoes with
Streusel Topping
Maple Corn Fritters
Red and Green Noodles
Greens and Cheese
Curried Greens
Curried Wild Rice Pilaf
Maple Glazed Lima Beans
Nutty Green Beans
Think Spring Greens
Stir Fried Summer Vegetables
Summer's Bounty Vegetables
Peas, Mint and Mushrooms
Golden Harvest Vegetables
Green Butter

Grandma always gently reminded us to eat our vegetables, and she knew how to prepare them so they were inviting and tasty. Vegetables help round out a meal by providing crunch and color. Welcome this addition of nature's bounty to your meals.

Country Style Lamb's Quarter

This is a family favorite, attractive and easy to prepare.

> **2 cloves garlic, chopped**
> **1/8 cup olive oil**
> **10 cups lamb's quarter leaves** (and seeds in season)**, rinsed well and torn into bite sized pieces**
>   (substitute other fresh greens or fresh spinach if desired)
> **1/4 tsp. salt**
> **1 Tbsp. lemon juice**
> **1 cup chicken stock**
> **2 slices lean bacon, cooked crisp and crumbled**

In large heavy skillet, sauté garlic in oil for about 2 minutes. Add lamb's quarter, salt, lemon juice, and chicken stock. Bring to a boil and cook, covered, over medium heat approximately 8 minutes, or until liquid has been absorbed. Place in a serving dish, and sprinkle with crisp bacon pieces. Serve immediately. Makes 6 servings.

Cranberry Spiced Squash

2 large acorn squash
2 cups cranberry sauce
1 Tbsp. pure maple syrup
2 Tbsp. orange juice
¼ cup dried sweetened cranberries
¼ tsp. ground cloves

Cut squash in half, place on a baking sheet (cut side down). Bake at 375° F. for 35 to 40 minutes. Meanwhile, combine cranberry sauce, maple syrup, orange juice, dried cranberries, and cloves in a saucepan. Cook over medium heat for about 5 minutes.

When squash is cooked, scoop out seeds and discard. Remove squash from rind, add to cranberry mixture and blend until smooth. Spoon into serving dish. Serves 6.

Carrots in Mint Tea

½ cup strong mint tea (See page 31 for recipe)
1 lb. carrots, peeled and cut into 2-inch pieces
Butter
Fresh parsley, finely chopped

Combine tea and carrots in a saucepan; cover. Cook over medium-low heat until carrots are tender; drain. Arrange carrots in a serving dish. Serve with a pat of butter and a sprinkle of parsley on top. Serves 6.

Maple Mint Yams

2 cups yams, cooked in mint tea (See page 31 for mint tea recipe)
$^1/_2$ cup orange juice
3 Tbsp. butter
2 Tbsp. pure maple syrup
1 cup crushed pineapple
$^1/_2$ cup roasted, chopped hazelnuts

Combine cooked yams, orange juice, butter, and maple syrup in a medium bowl. With an electric beater, beat until fluffy. Stir in pineapple and place in a buttered baking dish. Sprinkle nuts on top. Bake at 375° F for 15 minutes. Serves 6.

Spiced Sweet Potatoes with Streusel Topping

This spicy, aromatic dish is great as is, or dressed up with cinnamon ice cream or sweetened whipped cream.

2 cups applesauce
1 tsp. cinnamon
$^1/_4$ tsp. ginger
2 cups sweet potatoes, cooked and peeled
$^1/_2$ cup dried sweetened cranberries

Spoon 1 cup applesauce into a medium baking dish. Sprinkle with $^1/_2$ tsp. cinnamon combined with $^1/_8$ tsp. ginger. Prepare **Streusel Topping** (below). Spoon 3 tablespoons of topping over applesauce and spices. Arrange sweet potatoes over this. Cover sweet potatoes with remaining applesauce, and sprinkle with remaining spices. Spoon remaining topping over all. Bake at 350° F. for 30 to 40 minutes. Makes 6 generous servings.

Streusel Topping

    1/3 cup firm butter
    1/2 cup brown sugar
    4 Tbsp. flour
    3/4 cup rolled oats
    1/2 cup hazel nuts

Place butter in a bowl. Cut in brown sugar, flour, rolled oats and nuts until crumbly.

TIP: To cook yams or sweet potatoes: Wash well, cut off tips. Place in saucepan, cover with water or tea. Bring to a boil and cook until tender. Peel.

Maple Corn Fritters

    1 cup flour
    2 tsp. baking powder
    2 eggs, beaten
    1/3 cup milk
    1 Tbsp. butter, melted
    1 1/2 cups whole kernel corn
    2 Tbsp. onion, minced
    Vegetable oil for frying
    Pure maple syrup

Combine flour and baking powder in a large bowl. In a separate bowl, combine eggs, milk, and butter; add to flour and stir just to moisten. Add corn and onion; stir to combine. Drop by spoonfuls into hot oil; fry 3 to 5 minutes, or until lightly browned. Serve hot with warm maple syrup. Serves 6.

Red and Green Noodles

Red Noodles

    2½ cups flour
    3 eggs
    1 Tbsp. vegetable oil
    2 Tbsp. tomato paste

Place flour in the center of a work surface. Make a well in the center of the flour.

In a small bowl, combine eggs, oil, and tomato paste. Pour into the center of the flour. Using your hands, blend all ingredients. Gather dough into a ball. Knead, adding more flour if necessary. Cover and let sit 30 minutes, then roll out onto a floured surface to ⅛ inch thick. Cut into ½ inch wide noodles. Toss lightly with flour to prevent sticking. Spread onto lightly floured surface.

To cook, heat 4 quarts water to boiling. Add noodles and boil until tender, but firm (about 1 minute). Drain quickly. Serve with desired sauce, in soups, or buttered, as a side dish.

Green Noodles

Use the same recipe as above, but substitute ¼ cup cooked, drained, and chopped, squeezed wild greens for the tomato paste.

Greens and Cheese

2 cups wild greens, cooked in chicken broth
1 small onion, chopped
2 beaten eggs
½ cup milk
½ tsp. oregano
½ cup shredded Mozzarella cheese
½ cup soft bread crumbs, buttered

Combine all ingredients except bread crumbs in a greased baking dish. Sprinkle bread crumbs over top. Bake, covered, at 350° F. for 15 minutes. Remove cover and bake an additional 10 minutes, or until top is lightly browned.

Curried Greens

6 cups torn wild greens
1 medium tomato, cut into chunks
½ cup plain yogurt
3 Tbsp. cranberry chutney (See page 116 for recipe)
½ tsp. curry powder
½ cup lambs quarter seeds

Place greens and tomatoes in a large bowl. Combine yogurt, chutney, and curry powder. Spoon over greens. Sprinkle seeds over top, toss, and serve. Makes 6 servings.

Curried Wild Rice Pilaf

This is a great dish for lunch or dinner. Add crusty bread and a salad for an easy tasty meal.

1 cup wild rice, uncooked
1 small onion, chopped
2 Tbsp. butter
3½ cups beef broth
¼ tsp. pepper
¾ cup fresh mushrooms, cut into pieces
¼ cup hazelnuts, toasted
½ cup dried sweetened cranberries
1½ tsp. curry powder
½ cup minced green pepper
1 tsp. grated orange rind

Rinse rice until water runs clear. Sauté onion in butter in a heavy saucepan. Stir in wild rice. Add beef broth and pepper. When liquid reaches a boil, cover tightly, and reduce heat to low. Simmer for 1½ hours, or until liquid has evaporated and rice is tender. Stir in mushrooms and cook an additional 2 to 3 minutes. Toss rice mixture with hazelnuts, cranberries, curry powder, green pepper, and orange rind. Serves 6.

TIP: To toast hazelnuts: Place nuts on baking sheet; place in 350° F oven and bake, stirring occasionally until toasty and browned (8 to 10 minutes). Rub with cloth or towel to remove skins.

Maple Glazed Lima Beans

2 medium onions, chopped
1/4 cup butter
2 cups cooked lima beans
1/4 cup pure maple syrup
Salt and pepper to taste (Optional)

In a heavy skillet, sauté onions in butter. Add lima beans, maple syrup, and season to taste. Heat through and serve immediately. Serves 4.

Tip: To cook lima beans, soak beans in water overnight. Drain, and cover with boiling water or stock. Cover, reduce heat and cook until tender.

Nutty Green Beans

1 lb. fresh green beans
3/4 cup chicken broth
4 slices lean bacon, cooked crisp and crumbled
4 Tbsp. sesame seeds, toasted
4 Tbsp. hazelnuts, toasted and chopped

Wash beans and break off ends. Place in a heavy saucepan with chicken broth. Bring to a boil, reduce heat and cook until beans are tender, about 20 minutes; drain. Place beans in serving dish, stir in bacon pieces, and sprinkle with toasted seeds and nuts. Serve immediately. Makes 6 servings.

Tip: To toast sesame seeds, place seeds in shallow pan in 350° F oven for about 10 minutes, or until lightly browned. Shake often to prevent burning.

Think Spring Greens

3 cups cooked dandelion greens
1/2 cup light cream
1 Tbsp. butter
1/2 Tbsp. horseradish
1/4 tsp. salt
1/8 tsp. freshly ground pepper

Combine all ingredients in a medium saucepan, heat through, and serve immediately. Serves 6.

Stir Fried Summer Vegetables

2 Tbsp. vegetable oil
2 medium onions, cut up
1 tsp. dried basil leaves, crushed
1 Tbsp. chopped parsley
1 clove garlic, minced
1 cup peeled and chopped Jerusalem Articoke
1 large green pepper, cut into strips
1 small zucchini, thinly sliced
1 cup chicken stock
1/4 cup soy sauce
1 tomato, cut up
2 cups cooked wild rice

Heat oil in skillet or wok. Add onion, basil, parsley, and garlic. Stir fry for 2 minutes. Add green pepper, Jerusalem Articoke, and zucchini. Stir fry for another 4 minutes. Stir chicken stock and soy sauce into vegetables. Add tomato; cook until heated through. Serve immediately over wild rice. Serves 6.

Summer's Bounty Vegetables

2 large tomatoes, cut into chunks
1 cup fresh mushrooms, sliced
2 cups assorted wild greens, cooked in chicken stock and drained
⅓ cup chopped chives
1 clove garlic, minced
2 eggs, beaten
½ cup seasoned bread crumbs
⅓ cup grated Parmesan cheese

Arrange tomatoes and mushrooms in a lightly greased baking dish. Combine remaining ingredients, reserving 4 tablespoons each of bread crumbs and cheese. Place this mixture over top of tomatoes and mushrooms. Sprinkle with reserved bread crumbs and cheese. Bake at 350° F. for 15 minutes. Serves 6.

Peas, Mint and Mushrooms

1 lb fresh mushrooms
2 Tbsp. butter
2 Tbsp. flour
⅓ cup mint tea (See page 31 for recipe)
⅓ cup milk
2 cups cooked fresh or frozen peas

In a skillet, sauté mushrooms in butter, then remove; set aside. Stir flour into butter in skillet and cook for 1-2 minutes over medium heat. Slowly add tea and milk. Bring to a boil, then reduce heat. Add peas and mushrooms and simmer for 5 minutes. Serves 6.

Golden Harvest Vegetables

3 large carrots, peeled and cut into pieces
3 parsnips, peeled and cut into pieces
2 cups chicken stock
3 medium potatoes, peeled and cut into pieces
2 medium Jerusalem Artichokes, peeled and cut into pieces
3 Tbsp. light cream
2 Tbsp. butter
Salt and pepper to taste
Nutmeg

Cook carrots and parsnips in chicken stock over medium heat for 30 minutes. Add potatoes and Jerusalem Artichokes. Continue to cook for another 20 minutes, or until all vegetables are tender and most of the liquid has been absorbed. Drain off and add back enough liquid to mash with vegetables. Add cream and butter, and season with salt and pepper to taste. Place in a serving dish and sprinkle nutmeg lightly over top. Serves 6.

Green Butter

$1/2$ cup parsley, finely chopped
3 cups wild greens, finely chopped
$1/2$ cup chicken broth
$3/4$ cup soft butter

Combine parsley, greens, and broth in a saucepan. Cook 5 minutes over medium-high heat. Drain, and squeeze out excess moisture. Add softened butter and beat well. Chill. Use with sauces and over vegetables.

Chapter 9
Desserts

Berries n' Cream
Biscuit-Topped Berries
Rhubarb and Strawberry Pie
Berry Cobbler
Fresh Blackberry Pies
Fruit Crisp
Berry Cake
Nickey's Cookies and Cream
Cranberry Juice Dessert
Holiday Cranberry Balls
Banana Hazelnut Bread
Nut n' Maple Pie
Maple Chiffon
Holiday Crepes
Nutty Maple Crispy Cookies
Hazelnut Dessert Cake
Caramel Hazelnut Frosting
Mint Pound Cake

The crowning glory to many meals, desserts are pleasing to everyone. Try one of these desserts with your next meal or party and enjoy the taste of the outdoors with familiar sweets.

Berries n' Cream

The most simple of all desserts is fresh fruit — wild berries in season. Try crushed berries, sprinkled with sugar. Serve in champagne or wine glasses and garnish with a dollop of sweetened whipped cream. This is an elegant, wonderful ending to a summer meal.

Biscuit-Topped Berries

6 cups mixed wild summer berries
(Juneberries, blueberries, strawberries, raspberries, blackberries)
3/4 cup sugar
1/3 cup mint tea (See page 31 for recipe)
1 cup flour
2 tsp. baking powder
1/2 tsp. salt
2 egg yolks
1/2 cup milk

Combine berries and sugar in a large saucepan. Crush berries lightly. Add tea, and bring to a boil over medium heat. Reduce heat; simmer 10 minutes.

Meanwhile, combine flour, baking powder, and salt. In a separate bowl, combine egg yolks and milk. Pour over dry ingredients, stirring just until evenly moistened. Do not over-mix.

Again, bring fruit mixture to a boil. Drop teaspoonfuls of biscuit batter onto boiling fruit, placing dumplings close together in a single layer. Cover tightly and reduce heat to low. Simmer for 20 minutes. Remove from heat, partially uncover. Let cool about 15 minutes. Spoon into dessert dishes and serve while still warm. Makes 8 servings.

Rhubarb and Strawberry Pie

Whoever discovered the lovely combination of rhubarb and strawberries was indeed a genius! This pie is easy and tasty. Serve with vanilla ice cream or a large dollop of cinnamon-spiked whipped cream.

- **Pastry for two 9" pies**
- **1/3 cup sugar**
- **4 Tbsp. flour**
- **3/4 tsp. cinnamon**
- **2 cups sliced rhubarb**
- **2 cups sliced wild strawberries**
- **1 Tbsp. butter**

In a medium bowl, combine sugar, flour, and cinnamon. Add rhubarb and strawberries to sugar mixture; stir just to combine. Transfer fruit mixture to a pie pan lined with pastry. Cut butter into small chunks and place over filling. Prepare strips with remaining pie dough; cover top of filling. Sprinkle sugar and cinnamon lightly over the top. Bake at 450° F. for 20 minutes, then reduce heat to 350° F. and bake for an additional 30 to 40 minutes. Serves 6 to 8.

TIP: If frozen sweetened berries are used, defrost slightly first and reduce sugar in recipe by one-half.

Berry Cobbler

4 cups fresh mixed wild berries
1 tsp. cinnamon
1/2 tsp. salt
1/2 cup water
1 Tbsp. lemon juice
3/4 cup flour
1 cup sugar
1/2 cup firm butter

Combine berries, cinnamon, salt, water, and lemon juice. Taste and sweeten berries with sugar, if desired. Place in a baking dish. Combine remaining ingredients including sugar; mix until crumbly. Sprinkle over berries. Bake at 350° F. for 40 minutes. makes 6-8 servings.

Fresh Blackberry Pies

1 cup flour
2 Tbsp. sugar
1/4 cup firm butter
1 egg yolk, beaten
4 Tbsp. water
3 cups fresh wild blackberries
Milk
Additional sugar for sauce
1 tsp. vanilla

Prepare crust by combining flour and 2 tablespoons sugar. Add butter; cut into the dry ingredients until mixture resembles coarse cornmeal.

Add egg yolk and water; mix just until moistened. Divide mixture into 6 pieces. Pat each piece into rounds about 5 inches in diameter. Spoon 12-15 blackberries onto one side of the circle. Fold over and crimp edges. Brush top of pastry with milk. Continue with remaining pies. Place in a 375° F. oven and bake for 20 minutes, or until crusts are lightly browned. Meanwhile, combine remaining blackberries (approx. 1½-2 cups), 4 tablespoons sugar, and vanilla in a saucepan. Cook over low heat for 10 minutes. Let sauce cool.

To serve: Top pies with a scoop of vanilla ice cream and drizzle with blackberry sauce. Makes 6 individual pies.

Fruit Crisp

When we lived in Kentucky, it seemed that every cook knew the recipe for fruit crisp. It was there that I learned the simple equation for the dough: 1 part flour, 1 part sugar, 1 part milk and ½ part butter. The rest of the recipe was so simple. This is a family favorite, especially when we can use fresh wild berries.

- **1 cup self rising flour** (If you use regular flour, add 1 tsp. baking powder and ½ tsp. salt)
- **1 cup sugar**
- **½ cup firm butter**
- **1 cup milk**
- **4 cups mixed fresh sweetened wild berries** (You can use fresh sweetened fruit or canned fruit, drained)

Combine flour and sugar and cut in butter. Add milk; mix just until moistened. Place in well-greased baking dish and top with berries, or other fruit. Dough will rise up over berries during baking. Bake at 350° F. for 30 to 40 minutes, or until bubbly. Serves 6-8.

Berry Cake

Very much like the popular pineapple upside-down cake, this easy dessert will be your favorite as soon as you taste it.

- 1/3 cup butter
- 1/2 cup brown sugar
- 2 cups mixed wild berries
    (Juneberries, blueberries, raspberries, blackberries, and raspberries)
- 1/3 cup butter, softened
- 1/2 cup sugar
- 1/8 tsp. salt
- 1/2 tsp. vanilla
- 2 eggs, beaten
- 1 3/4 cup flour
- 1 tsp. baking powder
- 1/3 cup mint tea (See page 31 for recipe)
- Sweetened whipped cream (Optional)
- Sprigs of mint for garnish (Optional)

In a heavy skillet, combine 1/3 cup butter and brown sugar over medium-low heat. Stir until melted and well combined. Remove from heat; cool slightly. Crush berries and place on top of the butter and sugar mixture. Set aside.

In a medium bowl, cream together butter, sugar, salt, and vanilla until light and fluffy. Add eggs and mix well. In a separate bowl, combine flour and baking powder, mix until well combined. Add dry ingredients to the egg mixture alternately with the tea, beating well after each addition.

Pour batter into the skillet over the berries. Bake at 350° F. for 35 to 40 minutes, or until toothpick inserted in center comes out clean. Remove from oven and invert on a serving platter. Serve warm in wedges with whipped cream if desired. Garnish with sprigs of mint. Serves 10-12.

Nickey's Cookies and Cream

This is a bit like strawberry shortcake, but the cookies add a different texture to the dessert.

Cookies
1 cup butter
$1/2$ cup sugar
$2^1/_2$ cups flour
2 pints wild strawberries, crushed and sweetened lightly
Lightly sweetened whipped cream

In a large bowl, beat butter until creamy, then gradually add sugar, beating until mixture is light and fluffy. Stir in flour slowly, until a soft dough is formed. Roll dough out onto a floured surface and cut into 2-inch cookies. Roll out extra dough to make additional cookies. Place onto ungreased cookie sheets and bake at 350 F. for 12 to 15 minutes. Cool.

To serve: Place a cookie in a serving dish. Top with berries and a dollop of lightly sweetened whipped cream. Makes 6-8 servings.

Cranberry Juice Dessert

2 cups cranberry juice
1/4 cup brown sugar
1 tsp. cinnamon
8 slices bread
1 cup dried sweetened cranberries
Whipped cream (Optional)

Combine juice, brown sugar, and cinnamon in a saucepan over medium heat. Cook for 20 minutes; set aside. Toast bread and cut into cubes. Lightly grease a baking dish and place half of the bread cubes over the bottom. Top with half of the dried sweetened cranberries. Layer remaining bread cubes and dried sweetened cranberries over that. Pour prepared cranberry syrup over all. Place a plate over the top, press down, and refrigerate overnight. Serve like pudding with whipped cream over the top, if desired. Makes 8 servings.

Holiday Cranberry Balls

1 1/4 cups sugar, divided
1 cup chopped hazelnuts, toasted
1 cup coconut, lightly toasted
1 cup sweetened dried cranberries
2 eggs beaten
2 Tbsp. rum

Preheat oven to 350° F. In a large bowl, combine 1 cup sugar and remaining ingredients; stir until well blended. Spoon into a greased 8 inch square baking dish. Bake 20 to 25 minutes, stirring occasionally. Remove from oven and cool about 10 minutes. Using damp hands, shape into 1-inch balls. Roll in remaining sugar. Makes about 2 1/2 dozen.

Banana Hazelnut Bread

Bananas lend a tropical taste to this dessert bread.

- ³/₄ cup sugar
- ¹/₄ cup brown sugar
- ¹/₂ cup butter, softened
- 4 very ripe bananas, mashed
- 1 egg, beaten
- 1 tsp. vanilla
- 1³/₄ cup flour
- ²/₃ cup wheat germ, toasted
- 2 tsp. baking powder
- ¹/₂ tsp. cinnamon
- ¹/₂ tsp. cloves
- ¹/₈ tsp. salt
- ¹/₂ cup sweetened dried cranberries, chopped
- ¹/₂ cup hazelnuts, chopped, toasted

Combine sugars and butter; mix until fluffy. Add mashed bananas, egg, and vanilla. In a separate bowl, combine the next 6 ingredients. Add dry ingredients to banana mixture, blending well. Stir in cranberries and hazelnuts.

Place in a lightly greased loaf pan (9" x 5"), and bake at 350° F. for 35 to 45 minutes, or until a knife inserted in the center comes out clean. Remove from oven and let bread cool in the pan for 5 minutes. Turn bread out of the pan and cool on a rack.

TIP: Toast wheat germ on a cookie sheet in a hot oven for about 5 minutes, shaking pan occasionally.

Nut n' Maple Pie

1 9-inch unbaked pie shell
3 eggs, well beaten
1 cup pure maple syrup
2 Tbsp. butter, melted
1 tsp. almond flavoring
½ tsp. cinnamon
¼ cup hazelnuts, chopped, toasted
1 cup pecans, chopped

Prepare pie crust and bake in a preheated oven at 425° F. for about 8 minutes. Reduce oven temperature to 325° F. Remove pie crust from oven and set aside. Meanwhile combine remaining ingredients. Pour into the pie crust and bake at 325° F. for 30 to 40 minutes. Cool before serving. Makes 8 servings.

Maple Chiffon

1 cup pure maple syrup
4 eggs, separated
¼ tsp. nutmeg
1 pint heavy cream, whipped

In a medium saucepan, heat maple syrup to boiling over medium-high heat. Remove from heat and cool slightly. Stir in beaten egg yolks, return to stove, and heat almost to boiling. Again, remove from heat and cool slightly. Stir in stiffly beaten egg whites and nutmeg. Fold in whipped cream. Pour into a bowl; freeze. To serve, spoon into pretty serving bowls or wine glasses. Sprinkle with additional nutmeg. Makes 6 servings.

Holiday Crepes

These delicate pancakes, filled with fresh berries are great for a light dessert. It is a tradition at our house to prepare these for brunch on Christmas Day. Make extra crepes to freeze for future use.

Crepes
- **2 eggs, beaten** (room temperature)
- **1 cup milk** (room temperature)
- **1 Tbsp. melted butter** (room temperature)
- **1 cup flour**
- **2 Tbsp. pure maple syrup** (room temperature)

Topping
- **1 Tbsp. cinnamon**
- **1 quart vanilla ice cream, softened slightly**
- **3 cups mixed fresh wild berries, crushed, & sprinkled with sugar**
- **Few whole berries for garnish**
- **Powder sugar**

Combine crepe ingredients in a blender and mix well. Set batter aside for at least 1 hour at room temperature, or store covered in the refrigerator overnight.

When ready to prepare crepes, heat a lightly greased, stainless steel frying pan, or special crepe pan, over medium heat. Pour in enough batter to thinly cover the bottom of the pan. Cook for 4 minutes. Loosen the edges of the crepe and peel off. Crepes will be flexible. Store covered, on a plate until ready to fill. (A sprinkling of powdered sugar between each crepe will prevent them from sticking together.)

Meanwhile, combine cinnamon with softened ice cream. Place ice cream back in freezer until ready to serve.

To serve: Place 2 tablespoons crushed, sweetened berries in the center of the crepe. Top with a large scoop of ice cream. Fold one side over, and then the other. Add another scoop of ice cream over the top. Garnish with whole berries. Serves 6 to 8.

Nutty Maple Crispy Cookies

Filled with hazelnuts and chocolate chips, these cookies won't last long in your cookie jar.

> 1 cup butter
> ½ cup brown sugar
> ½ cup pure maple syrup
> 1½ cup hazelnuts, toasted and chopped
> 2 cups flour
> ½ tsp. baking powder
> 1 cup semisweet chocolate pieces

Combine butter and sugar. Add maple syrup, beat well. Stir in hazelnuts. In a large bowl, combine flour and baking powder; stir into batter; mix well. Drop by spoonfuls onto ungreased cookie sheets. Bake at 350° F. for approximately 10 minutes, or until lightly browned. Remove from cookie sheet and cool on racks. Makes 24 large cookies.

TIP: Hazelnuts are members of the filbert family. Filberts can be used interchangeably with hazelnuts and can be found in the baking section of most supermarkets.

Hazelnut Dessert Cake

Definitely not for everyday fare, this rich dessert combines elegance with great taste.

- ½ cup butter
- 2 cups sugar
- 4 eggs, well beaten
- ½ cup milk
- 1¾ cups flour
- 2 tsp. baking powder
- 2 cups finely chopped, toasted hazelnuts

Cream butter and sugar. Add eggs and beat well. Add milk and beat for 2 minutes. In a separate bowl, combine flour and baking powder. Add to egg mixture, mixing well. Pour into a well-greased and floured bundt pan. Bake at 325° F. for 1¼ hours. Cool 5 minutes in pan before turning onto cake plate. Frost with **Caramel Hazelnut Frosting** after cake has completely cooled. Garnish with crystallized rose petals (see page 111 for recipe).

Caramel Hazelnut Frosting

- 1 cup brown sugar
- ½ cup heavy cram
- ½ Tbsp butter
- ½ tsp. vanilla
- 2 Tbsp hazelnuts, **chopped and toasted**

Combine brown sugar and cream in a medium saucepan. Cook over medium-high heat for 8 minutes. Remove from heat; add butter and vanilla. Beat until thick. Frost cake and sprinkle nuts over top. (*This is more like a thick glaze which hardens as it cools.*)

Mint Pound Cake

Just a hint of mint and lemon gives this wonderful cake a mysterious flavor and aroma. Use in place of shortcake as a base for berries.

- 1/2 cup butter, softened
- 1/2 cup sugar
- 2 eggs, at room temperature
- 1 cup flour
- 1/2 tsp. baking powder
- 2 Tbsp. strong mint tea (See page 31 for recipe)
- 1 Tbsp. *lemon zest

Spray 2 small loaf pans with cooking spray. In a medium bowl, cream together butter and sugar until light and fluffy. Add eggs; beat well. In a separate bowl, combine flour and baking powder. Gradually add dry ingredients to butter mixture, beating well. Stir in tea and lemon zest. Spoon batter into prepared pans.

Bake at 325° F. approximately 25 minutes for small loaves, and 45 minutes for a larger loaf. Remove from oven and cool 10 minutes in pans. Remove from pans and cool loaves on rack. Makes 1 regular size loaf or 2 small loaves.

Tip: To obtain the best lemons, select those with a rich yellow color and a smooth, thin skin. Wash and grate only the outer skin to obtain fresh lemon zest.

Chapter 10
Miscellaneous

Snow Ice Cream
Berry Ice
Crystallized Rose Petals
or Mint Leaves
Rose Petal Frost
Rose Hip Syrup
Spiced Berry Syrup
Lemon Curd
Yogurt Cheese
Fragrant Potpourri
Chocolate Lovers Candy
Maple Baked Apples
Maple Crunchies
Cranberry Chutney
Tangy Cranberry Relish
Holiday Relish
Holiday Spiced Cranberry Sauce
Raspberry Sauce

Snow Ice Cream

This is a treat we look forward to every year when the first substantial snowfall arrives.

Lots of clean, fresh snow
1 cup cream (or milk)
$1/2$ to 1 cup of sugar (depending on your taste)
$1/2$ tsp. vanilla
(You can substitute any flavoring here. I have used both almond flavoring and maple syrup and found either to be very tasty.)

Send a reliable person out to gather the snow. In a large bowl or pot, combine cream, sugar, and vanilla. Add snow, one cup at time, beating after each addition. When mixture becomes very thick, it is ready to be enjoyed. You can adapt this recipe by using other flavorings, or by adding fruit or berries.

Berry Ice

4 cups fresh wild berries
$1/2$ cup pure maple syrup
1 cup Northwoods Tea (See page 31 for recipe)
2 Tbsp. fresh lemon juice

Mash berries and strain to remove any seeds. Combine with remaining ingredients and place in a shallow pan. Freeze for about 2 hours, stirring occasionally. Serve in sherbet dishes for a refreshing summer treat.

This can also be used as the basis for a tasty summer drink. Add water or juice to the ice in a frosty glass, stir, and garnish with mint leaves.

Crystallized Rose Petals or Mint Leaves

12 fresh rose petals or mint leaves
1 egg white
½ cup sugar

Wash petals or leaves and dry on a paper towel. Meanwhile, beat egg white until peaks form. Coat each petal or leaf with egg white, using your fingertips or a small artist's brush, then coat with sugar. Preheat oven to 225° F. Arrange petals or leaves in a single layer on a wire rack placed over a cookie sheet. Dry petals and leaves for about 15 minutes, keeping oven door slightly ajar. Store in a tightly covered jar in the refrigerator. Use as a garnish for summer drinks, desserts and salads.

Rose Petal Frost

3 cups mint tea
⅓ cups sugar
¾ cup orange juice
⅓ cup rose hip syrup (See following recipe)
3 Tbsp. orange rind
Chopped nuts for garnish

Combine tea and sugar in medium saucepan. Bring to a boil, stirring constantly. Reduce heat and simmer for 8 to 10 minutes. Add remaining ingredients and simmer for about 10 more minutes. Remove from heat and let cool. Place in a shallow pan and set in the freezer. Freeze 3 to 4 hours, stirring mixture occasionally to blend ice. Serve in pretty dishes garnished with chopped nuts. Makes 6 servings.

Rose Hip Syrup

2 cups fresh or 1 cup dried rose hips
½ cup apple, finely chopped (core but do not peel)
1 cup freshly picked mint leaves
2 cups Northwoods Tea (See page 31 for recipe)
2 cups sugar

Combine rose hips, mint, apple and tea in saucepan. Cook over low heat, stirring occasionally for about 1 hour. Strain. Add sugar to liquid and bring to a boil. Reduce heat and boil lightly for 15 minutes, stirring constantly to prevent syrup from sticking to the pan. Store syrup in refrigerator until ready for use. Makes 1½ cups of syrup.

Spiced Berry Syrup

Berry syrup is a natural over waffles, pancakes, ice cream or cake. Or, add water to make a wonderful spiced berry juice.

7 to 8 cups ripe mixed wild berries
1 cup mint tea (See page 31 for recipe)
4 cups sugar
¼ tsp. mace
1 Tbsp. cinnamon
½ tsp. allspice
½ tsp. cloves
2 Tbsp. fresh lemon juice

Mash berries; stir in tea. Heat to boiling over medium heat. Reduce heat to low, and simmer gently for 10 minutes, stirring occasionally. Strain, discarding seeds and pulp. Add remaining ingredients and simmer until mixture thickens slightly. Store in the refrigerator.

Lemon Curd

This excellent addition to freshly baked scones is enjoying popularity in coffee shops across the country. Great over biscuits or shortbread, too!

- **⅓ cup butter, melted**
- **1¼ cup sugar**
- **¼ cup powdered sugar**
- **1 cup fresh lemon juice**
- **⅛ cup strong mint tea** (See page 31 for recipe)
- **4 eggs, beaten**
- **2 Tbsp. lemon peel**

In medium saucepan, combine all ingredients. Cook over medium heat for about 30 minutes, stirring constantly. Mixture will become thick, much like the filling in a lemon pie. Serve warm or cold. This will keep well in the refrigerator. Makes about 4 cups.

Yogurt Cheese

- **2 cups plain or vanilla yogurt** (use vanilla yogurt if your cheese will be used with berries or with a sweet dish)

Place yogurt in a colander which has been lined with cotton cheesecloth. Place the colander over a large glass bowl. Set in the refrigerator and allow the yogurt to drain. This will take at least 12 hours. What will be left in the cheesecloth is very much like cream cheese. I use this on crackers, in dips, or almost any way that I would use regular cream cheese.

To store, simply wrap in plastic wrap and store in the refrigerator. Yogurt Cheese makes an exceptional treat when combined with fresh berries.

Fragrant Potpourri

Gather pine cones, birch bark, sweet fern, leaves from raspberry, strawberry, blackberry and blueberry bushes, wintergreen leaves and berries, clover blossoms, clover leaves, rose hips, dried rose petals, rose leaves, and/or any other items from the outdoors that you like, and think would compliment your mixture. Purchase Orris Root Powder or rose oil from your health food store, specialty shop or food co-op.

2 Tbsp. Orris root powder/rose oil
1 tsp. whole cloves
3 or 4 cinnamon sticks
any combination of the following:
> pine cones, birch bark, sweet fern, dried leaves from raspberry, strawberry, blackberry and/or blueberry bushes (see note for drying petals and leaves), wintergreen leaves and berries, clover blossoms and leaves, rose hips, dried rose petals, rose leaves, and any other fragrant items from the outdoors that will add scent to your mixture

Combine the orris root powder or rose oil with cloves and cinnamon sticks and 2 cups of a mixture of the remaining ingredients. To store, place in a tightly covered jar, or plastic bag, tightly sealed.

To use, place in a pretty container and use anywhere a fresh outdoor scent is desired.

NOTE: To dry leaves or flower petals, Place freshly picked leaves or petals on a baking sheet. Heat in 200° F. oven with the oven door slightly ajar for 2 to 3 hours. Stir petals or leaves occasionally. Cool. ***If dried leaves and petals will be used for teas. (DO NOT USE ORRIS ROOT POWDER OR ROSE OIL.)***

Chocolate Lovers Candy

$2/3$ cup milk
4 oz. unsweetened baking chocolate, broken into pieces
$2½$ cups powdered sugar
1 tsp. vanilla
1 Tbsp. Amaretto liqueur
2 egg yolks, beaten
$1½$ cups hazelnuts, toasted and chopped

Combine milk and chocolate in a heavy saucepan over medium heat. Stir, reducing heat if needed, until chocolate is melted. Add sugar, vanilla and liqueur and continue to stir until well blended. Remove from heat, let cool slightly and add egg yolks. Beat well. Transfer mixture to a shallow pan and place in refrigerator to cool, about 1 hour.

Remove from refrigerator and form into balls $½$ to 1 inch in diameter. Roll in crushed hazelnuts. Chill well. Makes about $1½$ dozen candies.

Maple Baked Apples

4 medium apples, cored but not peeled
4 Tbsp. pure maple syrup
$½$ cup sweetened dried cranberries
$½$ tsp. cinnamon

Core apples and place in a baking dish. Drizzle maple syrup in the center of each apple. Sprinkle cranberries in the center of each apple and add cinnamon. Bake for 30 minutes at 350° F., occasionally spooning syrup over apples. Serves 4.

Maple Crunchies

6 cups puffed wheat cereal
$1/2$ cup dried sweetened cranberries
2 cups hazelnuts, toasted and chopped
$1/2$ cup brown sugar
$1/4$ cup pure maple syrup
$1/4$ cups butter

Combine cereal, cranberries and hazelnuts in shallow baking pan. Meanwhile, combine sugar, maple syrup, and butter in a saucepan over low heat. Cook, stirring occasionally, until smooth. Pour over cereal mixture and toss to coat well.

Bake at 375° F. for about 45 minutes, stirring occasionally. Cool, break into pieces. Store in a tightly covered container in a cool place. Serve as a snack, or sprinkled over vanilla ice cream. Makes approx. 8 cups.

Cranberry Chutney

$1/4$ cup apple juice
1 cup fresh cranberries
$1/4$ cup apple, pared and grated
1 Tbsp. minced onion
2 Tbsp. brown sugar
1 orange, segmented and chopped

Place juice in a medium saucepan and add cranberries. Simmer over medium-low heat for 10 minutes. Add remaining ingredients; cook for an additional 10 minutes. Makes 1 cup chutney. Store in the refrigerator.

Tangy Cranberry Relish

2 cups fresh cranberries
1 orange
½ cup sugar

Place all ingredients in a blender container including orange peel and blend until relish is well chopped. Store in the refrigerator. Makes about 2½ cups relish.

This relish is best when made a day before serving.

Holiday Relish

This easy-to-make relish is a delightful addition to any meal. It also makes a wonderful gift.

4 cups whole, fresh cranberries, partially frozen
1 medium orange
1 medium apple, cored
1 medium lemon
½ cup brown sugar
1 tsp. ground cinnamon
¼ tsp. ground allspice

Wash cranberries. Chop coarsely in a blender, then place in a bowl. Wash orange, apple, and lemon; cut into quarters but do not peel. Remove seeds, cut into smaller pieces and chop in the blender. Add to the cranberries. Add sugar and spices; blend. Remove from heat and cool. Store in the refrigerator. Makes about 6 cups relish.

Holiday Spiced Cranberry Sauce

1½ cups pure maple syrup
¼ cup orange juice
2 cinnamon sticks
6 whole cloves
1 tsp. ground ginger
¼ tsp. nutmeg
4 cups fresh cranberries

Combine syrup, juice, and spices in saucepan and bring to a boil. Reduce heat and cook for about 30 minutes, stirring occasionally. Remove cinnamon sticks and cloves. Add cranberries and simmer until cranberries begin to pop, about 8 to 10 minutes. Remove from heat and cool. Store in the refrigerator. Makes 4 cups sauce.

Raspberry Sauce

1 pint fresh wild raspberries
¼ cup cranberry juice
1 Tbsp. sugar

Place berries and juice in a blender and process until puréed. Strain. Add sugar and stir to blend. Store in the refrigerator. Makes 2 cups sauce.

Index

Appetizers, 17-26
  Berry Good, 18
  Bread Pudding Squares, 25
  Cranberry Ham Spread, 19
  Creamy Green Dip, 20
  Crispy Green Crackers, 21
  Frosty Blue Ice, 18
  Fruit Appetizer, 24
  Lemon Mint Sauce, 25
  Northwoods Snack Slices, 22
  Raspberry Orange Toast Triangles, 23
  Saucy Relish, 19
  Summer Taste Treats, 22
  Terra's Tea Crescents, 26
  TLC Roll Ups, 23
  Wild Rice Balls, 21
  Zesty Cranberry Dip, 20
  Zesty Fruit Dip, 24

Berries
  Blackberries, 2
    Fresh Blackberry Pies, 98
    Hot Spiced Blackberry Tea, 30
    Lemons and Berries, 32
  Blueberries, 3
    Blueberry Pancakes, 38
    Frosty Blue Ice, 18
    Blueberry Muffins, 44
    Blueberry Sauce, 45
    Blueberry Soup, 65
  Cranberries, 5
    Autumn Nut & Cranberry Salad, 50
    Banana Hazelnut Bread, 103
    Blueberry Soup, 65
    Bread Pudding Squares, 25
    Chilled Cranberry Soup, 66
    Cranberry Chutney, 116
    Cranberry Ham Spread, 19
    Cranberry Juice Dessert, 102
    Cranberry Mint Punch, 28
    Cranberry Spiced Squash, 85
    Curried Wild Rice Pilaf, 90
    Double Cranberry Tea Bread, 42
    Holiday Bread, 37
    Holiday Cranberry Balls, 102
    Holiday Relish, 117
    Holiday Spiced Cranberry Sauce, 118
    Lemon-Hazelnut Scones, 47
    Northwoods Snack Slices, 22
    Maple Baked Apples, 115
    Maple Cranberry Ham Bake, 74
    Maple Gingerbread, 48
    Mulled Warm-Up Tea, 30
    Northwoods Meatballs, 75
    Oven Stew, 78
    Saucy Relish, 19
    Spiced Sweet Potatoes with Streusel Topping, 86
    Tangy Cranberry Relish, 117
    TLC Roll Ups, 23
    Zesty Cranberry Dip, 20
    Zesty Fruit Dip, 24
  Juneberries, 8
  Mixed Berries
    Berries n' Cream, 96
    Berry Cake, 100
    Berry Cobbler, 98
    Berry Good, 18
    Berry Ice, 110
    Biscuit-Topped Berries, 96
    Fruit Appetizer, 24
    Fruit Crisp, 99
    Holiday Crepes, 105
    Marinated Fruit Salad, 52
    Melon and Berry Salad, 52
    Spiced Berry Syrup, 112
    Summer Fruit Salad, 53
  Raspberries, 13
    Raspberry and Rose Hip Soup, 64
    Raspberry Orange Cooler, 33
    Raspberry Orange Dressing, 54
    Raspberry Orange Toast Triangles, 23
    Raspberry Sauce, 118

Index

Strawberries, 16
  Holiday Punch, 32
  Nickey's Cookies and Cream, 101
  Rhubarb and Strawberry Pie, 97
  Summer Strawberry Soup, 65
  Strawberry Butter, 40
  Strawberry Cream, 34
  Strawberry Fruit Salad Dressing, 54
  Terra's Tea Crescents, 26

Beverages, 27-34
  Chilled Rose Hip Cooler, 33
  Cranberry Mint Punch, 28
  Holiday Punch, 32
  Hot Spiced Blackberry Tea, 30
  Hot Spiced Wine, 31
  Lemons and Berries, 32
  Maple Mint Sodas, 29
  Minty Hot Chocolate, 29
  Mulled Warm-Up Tea, 30
  Raspberry Orange Cooler, 33
  Strawberry Cream, 34
  Very Northwoods Tea, 31

Butters, Spreads
  Green Butter, 94
  Honey Butter, 41
  Lemon Curd, 113
  Strawberry Butter, 40
  Yogurt Cheese, 113

Breads, 35-48
  Banana Hazelnut Bread, 103
  Biscuits and Strawberry Butter, 40
  Blueberry Muffins, 44
  Blueberry Pancakes, 38
  Holiday Bread, 37
  Clover Blossom Fritters, 46
  Double Cranberry Tea Bread, 42
  Fry Bread, 41
  Homemade Croutons, 38
  Homemade French Bread, 36
  Hot Scones with Blueberry Sauce, 45
  Lemon-Hazelnut Scones, 47
  Maple Gingerbread, 48
  Mapley French Toast, 42
  Quick Minty Muffins, 46
  Southern Cornbread Goes North, 39
  Tasty Wheat Muffins, 43

Clover, 4
  Clover Blossom Fritters, 46
  Clover Tea (Very Northwoods Tea), 31

Dandelions, 6
  Gingered Green Salad, 51
  Spring Soup, 64
  Tangy Dandelion & Pepper Salad, 56
  Think Spring Greens, 92
  Wilted Spring Greens, 58

Desserts, 95-108
  Banana Hazelnut Bread, 103
  Berries n' Cream, 96
  Berry Cake, 100
  Berry Cobbler, 98
  Biscuit-Topped Berries, 96
  Caramel Hazelnut Frosting, 107
  Cranberry Juice Dessert, 102
  Fresh Blackberry Pies, 98
  Fruit Crisp, 99
  Hazelnut Dessert Cake, 107
  Holiday Cranberry Balls, 102
  Holiday Crepes, 105
  Maple Chiffon, 104
  Mint Pound Cake, 108
  Nickey's Cookies and Cream, 101
  Nut n' Maple Pie, 104
  Nutty Maple Crispy Cookies, 106
  Rhubarb and Strawberry Pie, 97
  Snow Ice Cream, 110

Entrées, 69-82
  Chicken Fried Rice, 71
  Chilled Chicken and Wild Rice, 74
  French Bread Sandwiches, 77
  Grandma's Chicken & Dumplings, 72
  Grilled Chicken with Wild Rice, 70
  Individual Main Dish Pies, 76
  Maple Cranberry Ham Bake, 74
  Northwoods Meatballs, 75
  Northwoods Style Beans n' Rice, 79
  Oven Stew, 78
  Savory Summer Pie, 81
  Wild Rice & Roasted Chicken/Herbs, 73
  Wild Rice & Summer Vegetables, 80
  Vegetarian Chili, 82

Greens (also see Dandelions, Lamb's-Quarter)

Index

Autumn Nut and Cranberry Salad, 50
Creamy Green Dip, 20
Crispy Green Crackers, 21
Curried Greens, 89
Fragrant Green Soup, 66
French Bread Sandwiches, 77
Green Butter, 94
Green Noodles, 88
Greens and Cheese, 89
Individual Main Dish Pies, 76
Savory Summer Pie, 81
Summer Fruit Salad, 53
Summer's Bounty Vegetables, 93

Hazelnuts, 7 see Nuts

Jerusalem Artichokes, 9
Double Rice Soup, 63
Festive Vegetable Soup, 68
Golden Harvest Vegetables, 94

Lamb's Quarter, 10
Country Style Lamb's-Quarter, 84
Grandma's Chicken & Dumplings, 72
Spring Soup, 64
Summer Taste Treats, 22

Maple Syrup, 11
Berry Ice, 110
Holiday Crepes, 105
Holiday Spiced Cranberry Sauce, 118
Maple Baked Apples, 115
Maple Chiffon, 104
Maple Cranberry Ham Bake, 74
Maple Crunchies, 116
Maple Gingerbread, 48
Maple Glazed Lima Beans, 91
Maple Mint Sodas, 29
Maple Mint Yams, 86
Mapley French Toast, 42
Nut n' Maple Pie, 104
Nutty Maple Crispy Cookies, 106
Tasty Wheat Muffins, 43
Yogurt-Brown Sugar Dressing, 58

Mint, 12
Carrots in Mint Tea, 85
Chilled Vegetable, Bean & Melon Soup, 62
Cranberry Mint Punch, 28
Crystallized Mint Leaves, 112
Individual Main Dish Pies, 76
Lemon Mint Sauce, 25
Maple Mint Sodas, 29
Maple Mint Yams, 86
Mint Pound Cake, 108
Mint Tea, 31
Minty Hot Chocolate, 29
Mushroom & Green Noodle Soup, 67
Peas, Mint and Mushrooms, 93
Quick Minty Muffins, 46
Tabbouleh, 55

Miscellaneous, 109-118
Berry Ice, 110
Chocolate Lovers Candy, 115
Cranberry Chutney, 116
Crystallized Rose Petals, 111
Crystallized Mint Leaves, 111
Fragrant Potpourri, 114
Holiday Relish, 117
Holiday Spiced Cranberry Sauce, 118
Lemon Curd, 113
Maple Baked Apples, 115
Maple Crunchies, 116
Raspberry Sauce, 118
Rose Hip Syrup, 112
Rose Petal Frost, 111
Snow Ice Cream, 110
Spiced Berry Syrup, 112
Tangy Cranberry Relish, 117
Yogurt Cheese, 113

Nuts
Autumn Nut and Cranberry Salad, 50
Banana Hazelnut Bread, 103
Caramel Hazelnut Frosting, 107
Chocolate Lovers Candy, 115
Hazelnut Dessert Cake, 107
Lemon-Hazelnut Scones, 47
Maple Crunchies, 116
Maple Mint Yams, 86
Nut n' Maple Pie, 104
Nutty Green Beans, 91
Nutty Maple Crispy Cookies, 106

Potpourri
Fragrant Potpourri, 114

Index

Roses, 15
    Chilled Rose Hip Cooler, 33
    Crystallized Rose Petals, 111
    Raspberry and Rose Hip Soup, 64
    Rose Hip Syrup, 112
    Rose Petal Frost, 111

Salads and Dressings, 49-58
    Autumn Nut and Cranberry Salad, 50
    Crunchy Wild Rice & Yogurt Salad, 51
    Gingered Green Salad, 51
    Marinated Fruit Salad, 52
    Melon and Berry Salad, 52
    Olive Oil Dressing, 50
    Raspberry-Orange Dressing, 54
    Strawberry Fruit Salad Dressing, 54
    Summer Fruit Salad, 53
    Tabbouleh, 55
    Tangy Dandelion & Pepper Salad, 56
    Wild Rice Salad, 57
    Wilted Spring Greens, 58
    Yogurt-Brown Sugar Dressing, 58

Sauces, Relishes & Chutneys
    Blueberry Sauce, 45
    Cranberry Chutney, 116
    Holiday Relish, 117
    Holiday Spiced Cranberry Sauce, 118
    Lemon Mint Sauce, 25
    Raspberry Sauce, 118
    Saucy Relish, 19
    Tangy Cranberry Relish, 117

Soups, 59-68
    Beef Stock, 60
    Blueberry Soup, 65
    Chicken Stock, 61
    Chilled Vegetable, Bean & Melon Soup, 62
    Chilly Cranberry Soup, 66
    Double Rice Soup, 63
    Festive Vegetable Soup, 68
    Fragrant Green Soup, 66
    Mushroom & Green Noodle Soup, 67
    Raspberry and Rose Hip Soup, 64
    Spring Soup, 64
    Summer Strawberry Soup, 65
    Vegetable Stock, 62

Tea
    Very Northwoods Tea, 31
    Blackberry, 31
    Blueberry, 31
    Clover, 31
    Mint, 31
    Raspberry, 31
    Strawberry, 31
    Wild Rose, 31

Vegetables, 83-94
    Carrots in Mint Tea, 85
    Country Style Lamb's-Quarter, 84
    Cranberry Spiced Squash, 85
    Curried Greens, 89
    Curried Wild Rice Pilaf, 90
    Golden Harvest Vegetables, 94
    Green Noodles, 88
    Green Butter, 94
    Greens and Cheese, 89
    Maple Corn Fritters, 87
    Maple Glazed Lima Beans, 91
    Maple Mint Yams, 86
    Nutty Green Beans, 91
    Peas, Mint and Mushrooms, 93
    Red Noodles, 88
    Spiced Sweet Potatoes with Streusel Topping, 86
    Stir Fried Summer Vegetables, 92
    Summer's Bounty Vegetables, 93
    Think Spring Greens, 92

Wild Rice, 14
    Chicken Fried Rice, 71
    Chilled Chicken and Wild Rice, 74
    Crunchy Wild Rice & Yogurt Salad, 51
    Curried Wild Rice Pilaf, 90
    Double Rice Soup, 63
    Grilled Chicken with Wild Rice, 70
    Northwoods Style Beans n' Rice, 79
    Vegetarian Chili, 82
    Wild Rice & Roasted Chicken/Herbs, 73
    Wild Rice & Summer Vegetables, 80
    Wild Rice Balls, 21
    Wild Rice Salad, 57